Jakob J. Petuchowski is professor of Judaeo-Christian Studies at Hebrew Union College—Jewish Institute of Religion in Cincinnati, Ohio, the first such appointment at a rabbinical seminary. With an international reputation as a Jewish theologian and an expert in Jewish liturgy, he has made the Christian-Jewish dialogue one of his main preoccupations. He is the author or editor of twenty-six books (among them, **Ever Since Sinai, Prayerbook Reform in Europe,** and **Understanding Jewish Prayer**) and more than five hundred articles. Professor Petuchowski, who writes with equal facility in English, German, and Hebrew, published an earlier version of **Our Masters Taught** in German under the titles **Es lehrten unsere Meister** and **Ferner lehrten unsere Meister**.

Our Masters Taught

תנו רבנן

OUR
MASTERS
TAUGHT

Rabbinic Stories and Sayings

translated and edited by
Jakob J. Petuchowski

Crossroad · New York

1982

The Crossroad Publishing Company
575 Lexington Avenue, New York, N.Y. 10022

Printed in the United States of America

Library of Congress Cataloging in Publication Data

Main entry under title:

Our masters taught.

1. Aggada—Translations into English.
2. Judaism—Doctrines—Sources. I. Petuchowski,
Jakob Josef, 1925–
BM516.096 1982   296.1'9   82–9999
ISBN 0–8245–0521–2   AACR2

Fondly dedicated to my good friends,
the members of Temple B'nai Israel, Laredo, Texas,
who, since 1956,
have listened to my annual retelling
of what "our Masters taught."

Contents

III · About Life and Death

IV · About Revelation and Torah

V · About the Greatest Commandment

VI · About the Teachers of Torah

VII · About Prayer

VIII · About Righteousness and Charity

IX · About Husband and Wife

X · About Miracles and Merits

XI · About Redemption and the World-to-Come

Introduction

Essential and important as it is in certain circumstances to have a systematic theology, which has been worked out down to the last detail, one would also have to recognize that any kind of "systematic" theology is prone to suffer from at least two weaknesses. On the one hand, it is in the nature of most systematic theologians that they express themselves in the vocabulary and in the syntax of the dominant schools of philosophy, and that they are heavily influenced by the explicit and implicit assumptions of those philosophical schools—whether they are called Platonic, Aristotelian, Neoplatonic, Neoaristotelian, Cartesian, Idealistic, Existential or Logical Positivist. On the other hand, complete theological "systems" are liable to be perceived as "closed" systems, leaving no room for growth and new insights, and conveying the impression that what the theologian has put down on paper indeed exhausts the entirety of God's Truth.

On both of those counts, systematic theology has come in for a great deal of criticism within recent years. Philosophical fashions have been changing very rapidly—perhaps more rapidly during the last two hundred years than during the preceding two millennia. Modern systematic theologies tend to be "dated" very soon after their publication. Also, in an age of ecumenicity and religious pluralism, when one wants to be open to what is being said by those outside one's own religious communion, "closed" theological systems tend to stand in one's way—quite apart from the widespread acceptance of biblical criticism, which sees in biblical literature the "word of man" as well as the "Word of God," and which prevents the acceptance of any human theological construction as necessarily identical with the totality of Divine Truth.

In the light of such considerations, it has become fashionable of late in theological circles to look for ways of "doing theology" that would not impose the limitations and constraints to which systematic theology is necessarily subject. In the process, the discovery was made that not only a great deal of theology could be read as poetry, but also, and perhaps more significantly, that literature itself could serve as a vehicle for theology. The Bible is perhaps the best illustration of this. It does indeed furnish the theologian with essential raw materials, but it is not itself a work of systematic theology. The biblical authors convey their theology through storytelling, just as, later on, Jesus was wont to teach in parables. Our theological vocabulary has thus been enriched by the concept of "narrative theology," which, perhaps, is as yet still more talked about than actually practiced.

It is an attempt, of course, to penetrate to religious originality and inspirational immediacy. For the normal theology of the schools is a derived, a secondary, discipline. First comes the religious experience itself, an experience that finds its immediate repercussion in the stories of those to whom it had been vouchsafed. Only much later, when the immediacy of the experience is gone, or when the actual experience (revelations, miracles, etc.) is no longer repeated for subsequent generations, does the process of *thinking about* the primary experience and of systematizing those thoughts set in—particularly when a given religious communion has its traditions challenged by nonbelievers from without and by heretics from within. At that stage of religious development, we get the theologians and their systems, the dogmatists and their creeds.

The authors of the Hebrew Bible still lived in the first stage of that development, and so, to a certain extent, did the teachers of Judaism, the Rabbis, who flourished in the first six or seven centuries of the Common Era. (The first Jewish systematic theologian, Rabh Sa'adya Gaon, lived in the tenth century.) To hear them tell it, those Rabbis themselves, though no longer hearing the thunders and seeing the lightnings of Mount Sinai, still had experiences of a "Heavenly Voice" (to some of which, however, they could, on occasion, relate quite critically; see pages 43f.), of manifestations of the "Holy Spirit" and of the "Divine Presence" (*Shekhinah*), and of appearances of the Prophet Elijah, the Prophet who did indeed fly to heaven in a fiery chariot, but of whose actual death the Bible contains no report, and who, therefore, continued to function as a bearer of divine messages and as an almoner of divine charity.

Those Rabbis did, when the necessity arose, engage in theological debate with heretics from within the Jewish community, and with challengers from outside. After all, they lived at a time and in a place noted for the attractions of Near Eastern paganism, competing schools of Hellenistic philosophy, nascent Christianity and ever-seductive Gnosticism. But, for internal consumption, the Rabbis saw no need to develop a systematic theology. The late Professor Solomon Schechter was probably not far off the mark when he said of the Rabbis: "With God as a reality, Revelation as a fact, the Torah as a rule of life, and the hope of Redemption as a most vivid expectation, they felt no need for formulating their dogmas into a creed, which, as was once remarked by a great theologian, is repeated not because we believe, but that we may believe. What they had of theology, they enunciated spasmodically or 'by impulses' " (Solomon Schechter, *Some Aspects of Rabbinic Theology*. London: Adam and Charles Black, 1909, p. 12).

Spasmodically and impulsively or not, however, the Rabbis did, in fact, enunciate enough theology to cover most topics to which theology is expected to address itself. But they did not strive for theological consistency, nor did they compose theological tractates. In matters of law (*Halakhah*), both civil and religious, they aimed at uniformity of practice—albeit without the slightest desire to cut short debate. Legal decisions were arrived at by majority vote and/or authoritative decree. But, with only one or two notable exceptions, no attempts were made by them either to determine by a vote how a given belief is to be construed or to issue authoritative decrees as to what had to be believed.

Rabbinic literature offers us the greatest variety in statements of individual belief, without, in most cases, enabling the modern scholar to determine what, in fact, in all that diversity, was the belief of the majority, and what was the theological idiosyncrasy of an individual. It was a methodological error, therefore, on the part of nineteenth-century scholars like Ferdinand Weber, Wilhelm Bousset and others, to extract random theological statements from rabbinic literature, and, on that basis, to construct putative "systems" of the theology of the ancient Rabbis. A more likely way of arriving at the rabbinic belief structure is the method currently being developed by Professor Jacob Neusner, who takes authoritative *legal* texts as his starting point and then works his way back to the underlying assumptions. (See Jacob Neusner, *Judaism—The Evidence of the Mishnah.* Chicago: The University of Chicago Press, 1981.)

The nonlegal components of rabbinic literature are, in part, contained in the *Midrash,* i.e., the homiletical exposition of Pentateuchal pericopes and the so-called Five Scrolls (Song of Songs, Ruth, Lamentations, Ecclesiastes, Esther), but they are not confined to *Midrash* literature. They are also embedded to a very large extent within the legal literature of the Talmud. There, though they do occupy the same pages with legal matters (*Halakhah*), they are known as *Haggadah* in Hebrew, or as *Aggadah* in Aramaic. The word is derived from a verbal root that means "to tell" (the *Aggada* expounds what a Scripture verse "really means to tell us"), and also "to proclaim" (including the prophetic and eschatological sense of "proclamation"). It would, in many instances, not be too farfetched to render the word *Aggada* as "narrative theology."

Aggada is embedded in the *Mishnah,* the *Tosephta,* the Palestinian Talmud, the Babylonian Talmud, and in the so-called Tannaitic *Midrashim,* a literature stretching from the third to about the seventh centuries of the Common Era, as well as in the homiletical *Midrash* works, some of which are contemporaneous with the Talmud, and some of which may have been redacted as late as the tenth century. All of those writings purport to contain oral traditions, and some of their contents may indeed antedate the compilation of the *Mishnah* in the third century. It is from the entire range of this literature that we have selected materials for this volume. Neither the titles that we have given the individual narratives nor their arrangement by subject matter are inherent in the subject matter itself. They represent our own contribution to this venture.

Not wishing to fall into the methodological error committed by

Weber, Bousset and others in the last century, we want to emphasize that what is being presented here is not *the* theology of the ancient Rabbis. Instead, we are dealing with a proportionately small selection of texts that, for one reason or another, appeal to this editor—either because the thoughts expressed in them afford us an insight into the religious genius of the ancient Rabbis, or because one thought or another has, in the editor's view, a modern applicability, or, again, simply because the editor found a certain passage aesthetically enjoyable and hopes that the reader will share that enjoyment with him. It should be noted that, at least for some of the ancient Rabbis, enjoyment was nothing less than a virtue, the suppression of which could lead one into difficulties before God's Throne of Judgment. (See page 32.)

Those Rabbis were also convinced that, although the Sinaitic Revelation may have been *einmalig* (unique and meant for all times), man's perception of God's Word was anything but uniform. The same Scripture verse may give rise to different, and sometimes contradictory, interpretations—which, in spite of their contradictory nature, may be equally legitimate. Unlike God's Truth, man's truth is fragmentary, for man's understanding of truth is limited by his ability (see pages 37f.); and what, on the purely human level, may appear to be contradictory could still turn out to be fragments of the same Divine Truth, words of the same Living God (see page 41). This rabbinic insight has also guided us in our selection; and, as far as possible, we have tried to let this anthology reflect the diversity of views that the ancient Rabbis took so much for granted.

In a somewhat different arrangement, the stories contained in this volume have previously appeared in two German volumes, published by Verlag Herder in Freiburg im Breisgau, West Germany: *Es lehrten unsere Meister* (1979; fifth impression, 1981) and *Ferner lehrten unsere Meister* (1980). Although grateful acknowledgment is made to Verlag Herder for permission to let the stories now appear in an English garb, it should be pointed out that, for the purpose of including them in this volume, the stories have been translated anew, this time into English, from their Hebrew and Aramaic originals, and not from the previously published German translations.

As far as the present translation is concerned, every attempt has been made to convey something of the "flavor" of the original, for, at least some of the time, "the medium is the message." But rabbinic literature is often very cryptic and laconic, presupposing on the part of the reader an acquaintance with many other segments of that literature, and relying on the associative function of the reader's mind. That presupposition does not, of course, apply to the present volume. That is why we have occasionally incorporated explanatory comments in the texts themselves. At other times, we have omitted parts of the original, since the particular stories contained more than one point, and the reader, unfamiliar with this genre of literature, might lose the main point of a given story.

A "P." (or "p.") in front of a source reference denotes the Palestinian Talmud, whereas a "B." (or "b.") signifies that the selection was taken from the Babylonian Talmud.

Biblical quotations have been taken from the new English translation of the Holy Scriptures, published by the Jewish Publication Society of America (Philadelphia, 1962ff.)—except for some quotations from the Hagiographa (of which the Jewish Publication Society has thus far only published Psalms, Job and the Five Scrolls), and except for those instances where the rabbinic understanding of a verse quite obviously differed from that of the translators working for the Jewish Publication Society.

Throughout this book, one Hebrew word has been left untranslated. It is the word *torah*. The word means variously the "instruction" that parents give to their children, but also the "instruction" that *God* gives to *His* children. It means the "oracles" of the priests in the Temple, specified ritual "procedures," the "law codes" that have been incorporated in the Pentateuch, and also the Pentateuch as a whole. Such are the meanings already found in the Bible; and, for the Rabbis, *torah* can also mean the Hebrew Bible as a whole, that is, Pentateuch, Prophets and Hagiographa, as well as the "Oral Teaching," which, according to their belief, God revealed at Mount Sinai together with the "Written Torah." *Torah* is also that which individual Rabbis teach, as well as the way in which they conduct themselves. "Law" is *one* meaning of *torah*—alas, the only one that the Greek translators, using the Greek word *nomos*, managed to convey in the Septuagint. But "Teaching" is as much a part of the meaning of *torah* as "Law" is; and, since both

"Teaching" and "Law" were believed to have been given by God Himself, "Revelation," too, would be a suitable translation of *torah* in certain contexts.

Yet this is not all. *Torah* is not only the content of God's Revelation; it is also nothing less than the very blueprint according to which God created the world! (See pages 33f.) *Torah* is also what rabbinic Judaism is all about; and the reader will find references to it throughout this volume, and not only in Part IV, "About Revelation and Torah," and Part VI, "About The Teachers of Torah." *Torah* may have one specific meaning in one context and another specific meaning in a different context. But the overtones and the undertones of the word, derived from all of the contexts in which it appears, are audible also in any one of its specific meanings. That is why we have left the word *torah* untranslated. This whole book may serve as its lexicographical explication.

Jakob J. Petuchowski

Cincinnati, Ohio
Hanukkah 5742 / December 1981

· I ·
ABOUT GOD
AND THE GODS

What We May Say about God

The standard prayers of the Jewish liturgy did not yet exist in written form during the classical rabbinic period, and variations were common. Indeed, people were actually encouraged to "say something new" in their prayers every day. Within that setting, the following story is told.

A man once conducted the service in the presence of Rabbi Hanina. He began the Prayer of the Eighteen Benedictions as follows:

> *Praised are You, O Lord,*
> *our God and God of our fathers,*
> *God of Abraham, God of Isaac, and God of Jacob,*
> *great, mighty and awesome,*
> *majestic, strong, awe-inspiring,*
> *powerful, fearless, reliable and honored God!*

Rabbi Haninah waited until the man had finished; and then he said to him:

"Have you at long last exhausted all the praises of your Master? What is the use of all this? If Moses, in Deuteronomy 10:17, had not expressly written down that God is 'great, mighty and awesome,' and if the Men of the Great Synagogue had not expressly ordained the liturgical recitation of those three attributes, we

1

would not even be allowed to use those three. Yet you see fit to reel off all those others as well!

"This can be compared to a king of flesh and blood who had a treasure of one million golden denarii; and a man comes along, who praises the king for owning silver denarii. Would that king not feel insulted?"

B. *Berakhoth* 33b; cf. b. *Megillah* 25a

No Place Without God

A pagan once asked Rabbi Joshua ben Qareḥah: "Why of all things did God choose the humble thornbush as the place from which to speak with Moses?"

The Rabbi replied: "If He had chosen a carob tree or a mulberry tree, you would have asked me the same question. Yet it is impossible to let you go away empty-handed. That is why I am telling you that God chose the humble thornbush—to teach you that there is no place on earth bereft of the Divine Presence, not even a thornbush."

Exodus Rabbah II, 5; cf. *Numbers Rabbah* XII, 4

God Is No Thief

The Roman Emperor once said to Rabban Gamaliel: "Your God must be a thief, for it is written (Genesis 2:21–22): 'The Lord God cast a deep sleep upon the man and he slept; and He took one of his ribs and closed up the flesh at that spot. And the Lord God fashioned into a woman the rib He had taken from the man.'"

But the Emperor's daughter said to Rabban Gamaliel: "Leave him to me, and I shall answer him!"

Then she asked her father to order a captain of the guard to see her safely home.

The Emperor wanted to know: "Why do you need to be accompanied by a captain of the guard?"

She answered: "Thieves broke into our palace last night. They took away a silver jug, and they left us a golden jug in its place."

"Would that such thieves came to us every day!" the Emperor exclaimed.

"Precisely!" answered the daughter. "Was it not Adam's gain that he was deprived of a rib and received the gift of a wife, instead?"

B. *Sanhedrin* 39a

The Different Appearances

A heretic once asked Rabbi Me-ir: "How is it possible that He, of whom it is said in Jeremiah 23:24: 'For I fill both heaven and earth,' could speak to Moses from the small space between the two poles of the Ark of the Covenant?" (cf. Exodus 25:10–22).

Rabbi Me-ir said to him: "Bring me a convex mirror!"

The man brought it, and Rabbi Me-ir ordered him to look into the mirror.

He did what he was told to do, and he found his magnified image in the mirror.

Then Rabbi Me-ir ordered him to bring a concave mirror. Again, the man did what he was told to do, and Rabbi Me-ir ordered him to look into that mirror as well. When the man did so, he found a diminished reflection of himself in the mirror.

Now Rabbi Me-ir spoke to him: "You are only flesh and blood. Yet you are able to magnify or to diminish yourself according to your own desires. How much more so is He able to do that, through whose word the world came into being! If He so desires, He fills heaven and earth. And if He so desires, He can speak to

Moses from the small space between the two poles of the Ark of the Covenant."

Genesis Rabbah IV, 4, ed. Theodor-Albeck, pp. 27–28

The Suffering God

> *God called to him out of the thornbush.*
> (Exodus 3:4)

The Holy One, praised be He, said to Moses:

"Do you not feel that I am in pain just as Israel is in pain? Understand this from the place out of which I am speaking to you: the thorns! If one could possibly say so, I am sharing Israel's sufferings."

That is the reason why it is said in Isaiah 63:9: "In all their afflictions He was afflicted."

Exodus Rabbah II, 5

The Secret Promise

> *And God said to Moses: "I shall be present*
> *as the One who will be present." He continued:*
> *"Thus shall you say to the Israelites: 'I shall*
> *be present sent me to you.'"*
> (Exodus 3:14)

Rabbi Jacob bar Abina expounded this text in the name of Rabbi Huna of Sepphoris:

The Holy One, praised be He, said to Moses: "Tell the Israelites that I am with them in their present oppression, and that I shall also be with them in future oppressions."

But Moses replied: "Shall I really tell them that? Is the evil of the present moment not sufficient for them? Must I also speak to them about future oppressions?"

Then the Holy One, praised be He, answered: "No, tell the Israelites only that 'I shall be present' has sent you, but not 'as the One who will be present.' Only to you, but not to them, am I revealing the fact that there will also be future oppressions."

Exodus Rabbah III, 6

Your People

Rabbi Berekhyah taught in the name of Rabbi Levi:

There once was a king who owned a vineyard, which he entrusted to the care of a tenant. When the wine was good, the king used to say: "How excellent is the wine from my vineyard!" But when the wine was bad, he would say: "How miserable is my tenant's wine!"

The tenant, however, retorted: "Whether the wine is good or bad, it is, in either case, *your* wine."

Similarly, when the Holy One, praised be He, first spoke to Moses, He said: "Come, I will send you to Pharaoh that you may bring forth *My people,* the Israelites, out of Egypt" (Exodus 3:10).

But after the Israelites had committed the sin of the Golden Calf, He said to Moses: "Go down, for *your people,* whom you have brought up out of the land of Egypt, have corrupted themselves" (Exodus 32:7).

Moses then replied to the Holy One, praised be He: "Sovereign of the Universe, You apparently wish me to infer that, when the Israelites are sinning, they are *my* people, and that, when they are blameless, they are *Your* people. The fact of the matter is, however, that, sinful or blameless, they belong to You! That is why it is written in Deuteronomy 9: 29: 'For they are Your people and Your heritage.' "

Pesiqta deRabh Kahana, pisqa 16,
ed. S. Buber, p. 128b

God as Host

It once happened that Rabbi Eli'ezer, Rabbi Joshua and Rabbi Zadoq attended a banquet given by Rabban Gamaliel.

Rabban Gamaliel arose to serve them. He offered a cup to Rabbi Eli'ezer, who, however, refused to accept it. Then he offered a cup to Rabbi Joshua, and Rabbi Joshua took it.

Rabbi Eli'ezer now said to Rabbi Joshua: "Joshua, what is this? Are we to sit down and let ourselves be served by Rabban Gamaliel?"

Rabbi Joshua replied: "There was one even greater than Rabban Gamaliel who served others. Abraham was the greatest man of his generation. Nevertheless, it is written about him (in Genesis 18:18) that he stood up and served his guests. And don't tell me that Abraham knew that his visitors were ministering angels! He took them to be simple Arab desert wanderers. Why, then, should not we allow ourselves to be served by Rabban Gamaliel?"

At that point, Rabbi Zadoq spoke up and said: "How long are you going to invoke purely human examples? God Himself can be taken as an example! The Holy One, praised be He, causes the winds to blow, the mists to ascend from the earth, the rain to fall, and the earth to yield its produce. Indeed, He sets a table before everyone. Why, then, should we not let Rabban Gamaliel pour the wine for us?"

B. *Qiddushin* 32b

God Insists upon Truth

Moses had come and said: "The great, mighty and awesome God" (Deuteronomy 10:17).

Then came Jeremiah and said: "Strangers are destroying His Temple. Where, then, are His awesome deeds?"

That is why, in Jeremiah 32:17f., he omitted the attribute of "awesome."

Then came Daniel and said: "Strangers are enslaving His children. Where, then, are His mighty deeds?"

That is why, in Daniel 9:4ff., he omitted the attribute of "mighty."

But how were Jeremiah and Daniel able to omit something that Moses had ordained?

Rabbi Ele'azar said: "Because they knew that the Holy One, praised be He, insists upon truth, they were unable to utter any untruths about Him."

B. *Yoma* 69b

The Fear of God, Not of Men

Rabbi Samuel ben Sosratai once traveled to Rome, just at the time when the Empress had lost a bracelet.

He found the bracelet.

A herald traversed the Empire and proclaimed: "Whoever returns the bracelet within thirty days will receive a reward. But if the bracelet should be found in someone's possession after the thirty days, that person will be decapitated!"

Rabbi Samuel did not return the bracelet within the thirty days, but only after the thirty-day period had elapsed.

The Empress said to him: "Were you not in the Empire during those thirty days?"

He replied: "Yes, I was."

"Did you, then, not hear the proclamation of the herald?"

"Yes, I did hear it."

"And what did you hear the herald proclaim?"

He told her.

"Then why did you not return the bracelet within the thirty-day period?"

He replied: "So that you should not say that I returned it because I was afraid of *you.* I returned it because I fear *God.*"

And the Empress said: "Praised be the God of the Jews!"

P. *Baba Meẓi'a* II, 5,
ed. Krotoshin, p. 8c

In the Bath of Aphrodite

One day, Rabban Gamaliel went to bathe in the Bath of Aphrodite at Acco.

The philosopher Proclos met him there and said to him: "Is it not written in your Torah that you must not derive the least benefit from anything connected with prohibited idolatry? How, then, can you bathe in the Bath of Aphrodite?"

Rabban Gamaliel replied: "It is not allowed to have religious discussions in the bath."

When he had emerged from the bath, he said to the philosopher: "It was not I who ventured into the territory of the statue of Aphrodite. It was Aphrodite who came into my territory. After all, people do not say: 'The bath was made as an ornament for Aphrodite.' But they do say: 'A statue of Aphrodite was made as an ornament for the bath.' The prohibition mentioned by you refers only to such idols that are actually revered as gods. But that which is not treated as a god is permitted; and it is clear from all the physical functions that people perform in the bath that they do not treat the statue of Aphrodite as divine."

Mishnah 'Abhodah Zarah 3:4

Why God Does Not Abolish Idolatry

Our Masters taught:

The non-Jewish philosophers asked the Jewish Sages in Rome: "If your God does not approve of idolatry, why does He not simply abolish it?"

The Sages replied: "If people were to deify only that which the world does not need, God would certainly abolish idolatry. But people make gods of the sun, the moon, the stars and the planets. Is God supposed to destroy the whole world, merely because there are some fools around? No, the world continues in its accustomed course, and the fools guilty of corruption will one day have to render an account."

This is similar to the situation where a man robs a measure of wheat and then sows it. By all that is right, this robbed wheat should not sprout. But the world continues in its accustomed course, and the fools guilty of corruption will one day have to render an account.

B. 'Abhodah Zarah 54b; cf. Mekhilta, Bahodesh,
ch. 6, ed. Horovitz-Rabin, p. 226

· II ·
ABOUT GOD'S WORLD AND ITS HUMAN INHABITANTS

God Merely Supplies the Raw Material

The wicked Roman governor of Judaea, Tinneius Rufus, once asked Rabbi 'Aqiba: "Whose works are more beautiful, God's or man's?"

Rabbi 'Aqiba replied: "Man's."

Surprised at the Rabbi's reply, the governor said: "Can you, perhaps, make heaven and earth?"

'Aqiba responded: "Don't come to me with things that are beyond human power! Let us, instead, discuss something that human beings can accomplish."

'Aqiba then had ears of corn brought in from the field and beautiful, respectable loaves of bread from the bakery. He pointed to the ears of corn and said: "This is the work of God." Then he pointed to the bread and said: "And this is the work of man. Is it not more beautiful than the work of God?"

After this, 'Aqiba had bundles of flax brought in from the field and fine garments of Beisan manufacture. Again he called the natural product "work of God," and the manufactured product he called "work of man."

Then he repeated his question: "Is the work of man not more beautiful than the work of God?"

Midrash Tanḥuma, Tazri'a, 7, ed. S. Buber, p. 18a

"Worldly"

Rabh Huna once reprimanded his son, Rabbah: "Why is it that you are not attending the lectures of Rabh Ḥisda? They say about him that his teaching is very incisive."

His son replied: "Why should I go to him? Whenever I am there, Rabh Ḥisda only speaks of worldly matters. He lectures about the functions of the digestive organs and about other purely physical matters."

But the father said to him: "Rabh Ḥisda speaks of God's creatures, and you call that 'worldly'! Go to him!"

B. *Shabbath* 82a

Are You Seeking to Destroy My World?

At the time when the Romans were occupying Judaea, Rabbi Judah bar Ila'i, Rabbi Yossé and Rabbi Simeon bar Yoḥai were once sitting together. In their proximity sat Judah, the son of proselytes.

Rabbi Judah bar Ila'i began the conversation by saying: "How beautiful are the works of the Romans! They have built marketplaces. They have erected bridges. They have opened bathhouses."

Rabbi Yossé was silent.

But Rabbi Simeon replied and said: "Whatever the Romans have established, they have established for their own benefit only!

They have built marketplaces to settle prostitutes there. They have erected bridges to exact toll there. They have opened bath-houses to rejuvenate themselves."

Judah, the son of proselytes, reported that conversation to the authorities. Thereupon the government decreed: "Judah bar Ila'i, who has praised us, shall himself be praised. Yossé, who remained silent, shall be banished to Sepphoris. Simeon, who criticized us, shall be killed."

Simeon and his son hid themselves in the House of Study. His wife daily brought them a loaf of bread and a jug of water. But when the persecution increased, they became afraid, and they hid themselves in a cave.

There, a miracle happened to them. A carob tree grew for them, and a spring of water welled up for them.

They undressed and sat up to their necks in the sand. Daily they studied the Torah the whole day long. Only for the times of prayer did they get dressed, and after having prayed, they removed their clothes again, in order not to wear them out. In this manner, they remained in the cave for twelve years.

Then the Prophet Elijah came, stood at the entrance of the cave and called out: "Who will make known to the son of Yoḥai that the Emperor has died, and that his decree has been annulled?"

Hearing this, they left the cave.

When, passing an open field, they saw farmers ploughing and sowing, they became angry and said: "Those people are neglecting eternal life (i.e., the study of the Torah, which leads to life eternal) and are busying themselves with mundane matters!" And everything upon which they gazed was immediately consumed by fire.

Then a Heavenly Voice was heard, saying: "Have you emerged from your cave in order to destroy My world? Go back to your cave!"

> B. *Shabbath* 33b; cf. p. *Shebhi'ith* IX, 1,
> ed. Krotoshin, p. 38d, and parallels

Let Truth Spring Up from the Earth

Rabbi Simeon taught:

When the Holy One, praised be He, was about to create man, the ministering angels broke up into different groups and factions. Some said: "Let man be created!" But others said: "Let man not be created!"

Love said: "Let him be created, because he will perform deeds of loving-kindness."

Truth said: "Let him not be created, because he will be full of lies."

Righteousness said: "Let him be created, because he will act in righteousness."

Peace said: "Let him not be created, because he will be full of strife."

What did the Holy One, praised be He, do?

He took Truth and cast her down to earth.

At that, the ministering angels said to the Holy One, praised be He: "Sovereign of the Universe! Truth is Your seal. How could You put her to shame? Let Truth ascend again from the earth!"

That is why it is written in Psalm 85:12: "Let truth spring up from the earth."

To which Rabbi Huna the Elder, of Sepphoris, added: "While the ministering angels were still arguing about it, the Holy One, praised be He, created the man. He said to the ministering angels: 'Of what use is your discussion? Man has already been made!' "

Genesis Rabbah VIII, 5, ed. Theodor-Albeck, p. 60

A Single Human Being

For this reason a single human being only was created at the time of Creation: to teach you that whoever destroys a single life, Scripture reckons it to him as though he had destroyed a whole world; and whoever saves a single life, Scripture reckons it to him as though he had saved a whole world.

Also for the sake of peace among human beings, so that a man should not say to his fellow: "My father is greater than your father."

Also to prevent the heretics from saying that there are many divine powers in heaven, each one responsible for the creation of a different human being.

And also to proclaim the greatness of the Holy One, praised be He. If a human being stamps several coins with the same die, they all resemble one another. But the King of the kings of kings, the Holy One, praised be He, stamps all human beings with the die of the first man; and yet not one of them resembles the other.

Therefore every human individual is obligated to say: "For my sake was the world created!"

Mishnah Sanhedrin 4:5

The Last Creature

Our Masters taught:
Adam was the last creature created on the eve of the Sabbath. Why?
So that the heretics would not be able to say: "The Holy One, praised be He, had assistants in the work of Creation."

Another answer:
So that, if man gets haughty, he can be reminded that the gnats preceded him in the order of Creation.

Still another answer:

So that man, immediately upon being created, might embark upon the fulfillment of a commandment: the sanctification of the Sabbath.

And yet a further answer:

The completed Creation was a banquet, which God had prepared for him; and he was to go to that banquet immediately.

This can be compared to a king of flesh and blood who built palaces and furnished them. Only after they had been fully furnished did he prepare a banquet; and only then did he invite the guests. That is why it is said in Proverbs 9:1–3:

> *Wisdom has built her house,*
> *she has hewn out her seven pillars.*
> *She has slaughtered her beasts,*
> *she has mixed her wine,*
> *she has also set her table.*
> *She has sent out her maids*
> *to call from the highest places in the town.*

"Wisdom has built her house." That is an attribute of the Holy One, praised be He, who created the world with Wisdom. (See pages 33f., "In the Beginning Was Wisdom.")

"She has hewn out her seven pillars." Those are the seven days of Creation.

"She has slaughtered her beasts, etc." Those are the seas and the rivers, and everything else needed by the world.

"She has sent out her maidens to call, etc." That refers to Adam and Eve.

B. Sanhedrin 38a

Body and Soul

Rabbi Ishmael taught the following parable to explain the inter-relationship of body and soul:

A king owned an orchard with goodly figs, which ripen early. He appointed two watchmen, a blind one and a lame one, to watch over the figs. Then the king went away.

After a while, the lame man said to the blind man: "I see some goodly figs." And the blind man said: "Bring them to me, and we shall eat them!"

"What makes you think that I can walk?" the lame man said to the blind man; and the blind man replied: "And what makes you think that I can see?"

What did they do?

The lame man sat upon the shoulders of the blind man, and steered him toward the figs. They took the figs, ate them, and then returned, each man to his original position.

After some days, the king returned. When he did not see the figs, he challenged the watchmen: "Where are the figs?"

The blind man responded by saying: "Am I able to see?" And the lame man responded by saying: "Am I able to walk?"

But the king was clever. He placed the lame man on the shoulders of the blind man, and said: "That's the way you have done it!" Then he condemned them both together.

Thus, too, will the Holy One, praised be He, act in the eschatological future.

He will say to the soul: "Why have you sinned against Me?" And the soul will answer: "Sovereign of the Universe, *I* am supposed to have sinned against you? It was the body that has sinned! For, surely, I have not committed any sins ever since I have left the body."

Then He will say to the body: "Why have you sinned?" And the body will answer: "Sovereign of the Universe, it was the *soul* that has sinned! For, ever since it has departed from me, I have been before You like a lifeless potsherd that one throws upon the dung-hill."

What, then, is the Holy One, praised be He, going to do?

He will restore the soul to the body, and He will judge body and soul together, as a unified being.

That is why it is said in Psalm 50:4:

> *He summoned the heavens above,*
> *and the earth, for the trial of His people* (*Hebrew:* 'ammo).

"He summoned the heavens above"—to bring back the soul.

"And the earth"—to fetch the body; to judge the soul together with it (Hebrew: *'immo*).

Leviticus Rabbah IV, 5,
ed. Margulies, pp. 88–89

The Religious Obligation

The merciful man does good to his own soul.
(Proverbs 11:17)

This refers to Hillel the Elder.

Once, when he had concluded a class session with his disciples, he left the House of Study with them.

The disciples asked him: "Master, where are you going?"

He replied: "To fulfill a religious obligation."

"What is this religious obligation?" the disciples wanted to know.

He replied: "I am going to the bathhouse in order to have a bath."

The disciples were astonished, and they asked: "Is that really a religious obligation?"

He answered: "Yes! If the statues of the kings that are placed in theaters and circuses are daily cleaned and washed, and if the man whose job it is to clean and wash those statues not only makes his living from this, but also occupies an elevated position among the great ones of the Empire, how much more does this apply to me, seeing that I have been made in the image and likeness of God! For it is written in Genesis 9:6: 'In the image of God did He make man.' "

Leviticus Rabbah XXXIV, 3,
ed. Margulies, pp. 775–77

Freedom of the Will

Rabbi Ḥanina bar Papa explained:
The angel in charge of conception is called *Lailah* (the Hebrew word for "night"). When a conception occurs, the angel takes the drop of semen and places it before the Holy One, praised be He, and says: "Sovereign of the Universe, what is going to be the fate of this drop? Will it develop into a robust or into a weak person? An intelligent or a stupid person? A wealthy or a poor person?"
And God decides all of that.
But one question is not asked by the angel, nor is it decided by God: "Will it be a righteous or a wicked person?"

This follows the overall position of Rabbi Ḥanina; for Rabbi Ḥanina had taught: "Everything is in the hand of God, except the fear of God."

B. *Niddah* 16b

At the Moment of Conception

Antoninus asked Rabbi (Judah the Patriarch);
"When is the soul placed in man—at the moment of conception, or only after the embryo has been formed?"

Rabbi Judah answered: "When the embryo has been formed."
Antoninus objected:

"Can a piece of meat be kept unsalted for three days without putrefying? One would, therefore, have to assume that the life-sustaining soul is implanted in the human being already at the moment of his conception."

Then Rabbi Judah said:

"Antoninus has taught me this matter. Scripture actually supports him, when it says in Job 10:12: 'Your providence has watched over my spirit.' "

B. *Sanhedrin* 91b

Only from the Moment of Birth

Antoninus asked Rabbi (Judah the Patriarch):

"At what point does the evil inclination begin to have dominion over man—from the moment the embryo is formed, or only from the moment of birth?"

Rabbi Judah answered: "From the moment the embryo is formed."

Antoninus objected:

"If this were so, then the embryo would already rebel in its mother's womb and leave it. You will, therefore, have to say that the evil inclination begins to have dominion over man only from the moment of his birth."

Then Rabbi Judah said:

"Antoninus has taught me this matter. Scripture actually supports him, when it says in Genesis 4:7: 'Sin is crouching at the door.' "

B. *Sanhedrin* 91b

The Evil Inclination

The evil inclination within man is lusting only after what is forbidden.

On a Day of Atonement, when eating and drinking are strictly prohibited, Rabbi Mana visited Rabbi Ḥaggai, who was sick.

Rabbi Ḥaggai complained: "I am very thirsty."

Rabbi Mana said to him: "Seeing that you are sick, you may drink."

After a while, Rabbi Mana returned, and he asked Rabbi Ḥaggai: "How is your thirst?"

Rabbi Ḥaggai replied: "The moment you permitted me to drink, my thirst disappeared."

P. *Yoma* VI, 4, ed. Krotoshin, p. 43d; cf. Romans 7:8

Not Like the Ass

Rabbi Joshua ben Levi taught:

When the Holy One, praised be He, said to Adam: "Thorns and thistles shall the earth bring forth for you" (Genesis 3:18), tears flowed from Adam's eyes.

He said to Him: "Sovereign of the Universe, am I and my ass to eat from the same crib?"

But as soon as He said to him: "By the sweat of your brow shall you get bread to eat" (Genesis 3:19), Adam calmed down again.

Rabbi Simeon ben Laqish said: "Happy are we that God did not let the matter rest with the first decree!"

But Abbaye opined: "We did not escape that first decree altogether, for we still do eat the herbs of the field."

B. *Pesaḥim* 118a

Ecumenical Occasion

A certain Gentile asked Rabbi Joshua:

"You have festivals, and we have festivals. When you are happy, we are not happy; and when we are happy, you are not happy. Is there no occasion when we could rejoice together?"

"There is," replied Rabbi Joshua. "When the rain falls."

How can this be proved from the Scriptures?

From what it says in Psalm 65:14: "The meadows are clothed with flocks, the valleys mantled with grain; they raise a shout, they break into song." And immediately afterward (Psalm 66:2) it says: "Raise a shout for God, all the earth!"

It does *not* say there: "Raise a shout for God, you priests, Levites or Israelites!" But it does say: "Raise a shout for God, *all the earth!*"

Genesis Rabbah XIII, 6, ed. Theodor-Albeck,
pp. 116–17

They Are All Equal

I call heaven and earth to witness:

Whether Jew or Gentile, whether man or woman, whether manservant or maidservant, they are all equal in this: that the Holy Spirit rests upon them in accordance with their deeds!

Note: It is not unlikely that, at one time, the text had "freeman" instead of "maidservant." The contrasts implied by the other categories mentioned here seem to demand this. See also Galatians 3:28.

Seder Eliyyahu Rabbah 10, ed. Friedmann, p. 48

• III •
ABOUT LIFE AND DEATH

The Three Participants

It has been taught:

Three participants are involved when a child is formed in its mother's womb: the Holy One, praised be He, the father and the mother.

From the father come the white substances of the body, like the brain, the nails, the white of the eyes, the bones and the sinews.

From the mother come the red substances of the body, like the blood, the skin, the flesh, the hair and the black of the eyes.

The Holy One, praised be He, His Name be exalted, provides the following ten things: life-sustaining spirit and soul, facial expression, sight, hearing and speech, the ability to lift up one's hands and to walk with one's feet, and wisdom and insight, counsel, knowledge and strength.

When the hour of death arrives, the Holy One, praised be He, takes away His contribution and leaves the parents their contributions.

When the parents weep, the Holy One, praised be He, says to them: "Why do you weep? Have I taken away anything that belongs to you? I have taken away only what belongs to Me."

But the parents reply: "Sovereign of the Universe, as long as Your contribution was combined with our contribution, our con-

23

tribution was preserved from the maggot and the worm. Now that You have withdrawn Your contribution from ours, our contribution has been cast away and left to the maggot and the worm."

Ecclesiastes Rabbah V, 10, ii

The Seven Vanities

Vanity of vanities,
says the Preacher,
vanity of vanities!
All is vanity!
(Ecclesiastes 1:2)

Note: Rabbinic exegesis assumes that an unspecified plural must be understood as a minimum of two. The word *vanity* in Ecclesiastes 1:2 occurs three times in the singular and twice in the plural. This yields a total of "seven vanities."

Rabbi Samuel, the son of Rabbi Isaac, taught in the name of Rabbi Simeon, the son of Rabbi Ele'azar:

The "seven vanities," of which the Preacher speaks, correspond to the seven stages of a man's life.

When he is one year old, he is like a king who is carried in a canopied litter. All embrace and kiss him.

When he is two and three years old, he is like a pig that sticks its hooves into all the gutters.

When he is ten years old, he skips like a kid.

When he is twenty years old, he is like a neighing horse. He adorns himself and is looking for a wife.

After he has married, he slaves away like an ass.

When he has put children into the world, he becomes brazen like a dog, to supply their food and needs.

And when he has finally become old, he walks bent like an ape.

But what has been said here applies only to the ignorant. Of those who are well versed in the Torah, it is said of King David, for example: "King David was now old, advanced in years" (1 Kings 1:1). "Old" he was, but still a "king!"

Ecclesiastes Rabbah I, 2, cf. William Shakespeare,
As You Like It, Act II, Scene 7

"Give Me Company, or Give Me Death!"

Rabbi Yohanan taught:

All his life long did Honi, that righteous man, trouble himself to understand Psalm 126:1: "When the Lord returned the captivity of Zion, we were like those who dream." Since the Babylonian exile lasted seventy years, the verse would seem to imply that one could sleep and dream for seventy years. But did anybody ever sleep for seventy years?

One day, while he was walking on the road, he saw a man planting a carob tree.

He asked the man: "You know that it takes seventy years for a carob tree to bear fruit. Do you believe that you are going to live another seventy years, so that you can eat of the fruit of this tree?"

The man answered: "I have found a world with carob trees when I came into it. Just as my ancestors have planted carob trees for me, so I am planting carob trees for my descendants."

After this conversation, Honi sat down to eat. Sleep overcame him. While he was sleeping, a grotto was formed around him, so that he was shielded from the eyes of the people. He slept for seventy years.

When he awoke at last, he saw a man gathering carobs from the carob tree and eating them. He asked him: "Do you know who planted this carob tree?" The man replied: "My grandfather." "In that case," said Honi, "I must have slept for seventy years!"

. . .

He then went to his own home, and asked whether the son of Honi the Circle-Drawer was still alive. They told him that the son of Ḥoni was no longer alive, but that his grandson was. Then he said: "I am Ḥoni." But people did not believe him.

After that, he went to the House of Study and participated in the discussion. He heard the scholars say: "The material is as clear to us today as it used to be in the days of Ḥoni the Circle-Drawer. For, when Ḥoni came to the House of Study, he always managed to clear up all the difficulties of the scholars."

"But I *am* Ḥoni!" he cried.

They did not believe him, nor did they show him the respect to which, he felt, he was entitled.

Ḥoni now turned to God, appealing to His mercy and praying for death.

And he died.

Rabha said: "This is the origin of the popular saying: 'Give me company, or give me death!' "

B. Ta'anith 23a

The Fox and the Vineyard

> *As man came out of his mother's womb,*
> *so must he depart at last,*
> *naked as he came.*
> *He can take nothing of his wealth*
> *to carry away with him.*
> (Ecclesiastes 5:14)

Genibha said:

This can be compared to a fox who found a vineyard. But the vineyard was surrounded by a fence on all sides. The fox did indeed find a hole in the fence, through which he wanted to enter. Yet the hole was too narrow, and he did not succeed. What did he do? He fasted for three days, until he became quite slim; and thus he managed to get through the hole.

Then he ate the grapes. But, doing so, he again became fat.

That is why he did not succeed in getting through the hole when he wanted to leave the vineyard again. So he fasted for another three days to become slim; and, when he had done so, he managed to get out of the vineyard.

Once outside, he turned toward the vineyard and lamented: "O vineyard, O vineyard, how good you are, and how good are your fruits! All that is within you is beautiful and praiseworthy! But of what use are you? The way one enters you is also the way in which one leaves you again."

And so it is with this world!

Ecclesiastes Rabbah V. 14

The Place Where One Has to Be

There once were two Ethiopians who served King Solomon: Elihoreph and Ahijah, the scribes (1 Kings 4:3).

One day, Solomon saw that the Angel of Death was sad. He asked him: "Why are you so sad?"

And the Angel of Death replied: "Because I have been ordered to bring the two Ethiopians who are sitting here."

Thereupon Solomon commended his two servants to the spirits at his command and ordered the spirits to take his two servants to the district of Luz.

But as soon as they had arrived in the district of Luz, Elihoreph and Ahijah died.

The next day, Solomon saw that the Angel of Death was very happy. He asked him: "Why are you so happy?"

And the Angel of Death replied: "Because you sent your two servants to the very place from which I was expected to bring them."

Solomon then composed the proverb: "A man's feet are his guarantors. They lead him to the place where he has to be."

B. *Sukkah* 53a

The Banquet

Rabbi Eli'ezer taught: "Repent one day before your death!"

His disciples asked him: "But does one know on what day one is going to die?"

Rabbi Eli'ezer replied: "All the more reason, therefore, to repent today already! For it is possible that one might die tomorrow. And in this manner one would devote one's whole life to repentance. That is why Solomon said in his wisdom: 'Let your clothes always be freshly washed, and your head never lack ointment' (Ecclesiastes 9:8)."

Rabban Yoḥanan ben Zakkai used a parable for this:

This can be compared to a king who invited his servants to a banquet, without, however, telling them at what time the banquet would be held. The wise servants beautified themselves at once and waited at the gate of the palace. For they thought that the royal palace was lacking in nothing, and that the gate could be opened at any time.

But the foolish servants continued with their work. For they thought that a great many preparations would first have to be made for the banquet, and that it would take a while for the gate to be opened.

Suddenly the king demanded the presence of his servants. The wise servants entered all beautified, but the foolish servants entered in their dirty clothes. The king was very pleased to see the wise servants, but he was enraged at the foolish servants.

Then he commanded: "Those who have beautified themselves for the banquet should sit down and eat and drink! But those who have not beautified themselves for the banquet are to stand and merely watch!"

B. *Shabbath* 153a; cf. *Mishnah Abhoth* 2:10;
Ecclesiastes Rabbah IX, 8; Matthew 22:1–14

The Two Ships

The day on which a great man dies is better than the day on which he was born. For nobody knows on the day of his birth what deeds he is yet to accomplish. But on the day of his death, his good deeds will be made known to all. That is why "a good name is better than fragrant oil, and the day of death better than the day of birth" (Ecclesiastes 7:1).

Rabbi Levi explained:

This can be compared to two seagoing ships. One of them is leaving the harbor, and the other is entering the harbor. Everybody is celebrating the departing ship, but only a few are rejoicing at the ship that is arriving.

A wise man, seeing this, says: "One should have expected the opposite. People should not celebrate the departing ship. Who knows what is still ahead of it, whether it will sail through calm or stormy seas, and what winds it will have to face? One should rather rejoice over the ship that is entering the harbor, because it has safely returned from its voyage."

So it is when a man is born. Every day brings him closer to death. But once he has died, one hopefully begins to count the days until the Resurrection.

> *Exodus Rabbah* XLVIII, 1; cf.
> *Ecclesiastes Rabbah* VII, 1, iv

The Laborers in the Vineyard

When Rabbi Bun, the son of Rabbi Ḥiyya, died, Rabbi Zera delivered the eulogy. He took as his text Ecclesiastes 5:11: "A worker's sleep is sweet, whether he has much or little to eat."

I will tell you to whom Rabbi Bun can be compared.

A king had a vineyard. He hired laborers to tend it. Now, there was among the laborers one who worked better than all the others. When the king saw how diligently this laborer worked, he took him by the hand and began to stroll with him up and down.

But when, in the evening, the laborers came to receive their wages, the king paid that man as much as he paid the others.

When the other laborers saw this, they complained and said: "Your Majesty, while we have labored the whole day long, this man has only worked for two or three hours. Is it right that he should receive the same wages we do?"

But the king replied: "Why are you angry? This man has done as much work in two or three hours as the rest of you have done in a whole day."

Thus, too, Rabbi Bun has accomplished more in the realm of the Torah during his twenty-eight years than a diligent student could ordinarily accomplish in a hundred years.

Canticles Rabbah VI, 2; cf.
Ecclesiastes Rabbah V, 11, v; p. *Berakhoth* II, 8,
ed. Krotoshin, p. 5c; Matthew 20:1–16

The Reclaimed Treasure

One Sabbath, when Rabbi Me-ir was sitting in the House of Study in the afternoon, expounding the Scriptures, his two sons died.

What did his wife do? She laid both of them upon a bed and covered them with a sheet.

At the termination of the Sabbath, Rabbi Me-ir returned home. He asked his wife: "Where are my two sons?" She answered: "They went to the House of Study." But Rabbi Me-ir said: "I looked for them in the House of Study, but I did not see them there."

After he had been given the cup of wine for the prayer marking the termination of the Sabbath, and had recited the appropriate benediction, Rabbi Me-ir asked again: "Where are my two sons?" His wife replied: "They must have gone somewhere and must be coming home soon."

She then served him his dinner. He ate it and recited the Grace after Meals.

After he had concluded the Grace, his wife said to him: "Rabbi, may I ask you a legal question?"

"Of course, little daughter," replied Rabbi Me-ir, "ask!"

She related: "Some time ago, a man came here and gave me a treasure to keep for him. Now he has come again, this time to take it back. Must I return it to him or not?"

Rabbi Me-ir was quick to answer: "But of course, little daughter, you must return it to him. If one undertakes to keep something for someone, one must return it upon demand!"

She said to him: "Rabbi, do you really think that I would not do so—even without your ruling?"

Then she took him by the hand and led him upstairs to the room where the two dead sons were lying on a bed. She removed the sheet with which she had covered them.

When Rabbi Me-ir saw that his two sons were dead, he wailed and cried: "My sons, my sons! My Masters, my Masters!" ("My sons"—because they were so well behaved. "My Masters"—because they have enlightened me through their study of the Torah.)

Now his wife spoke to him: "Rabbi, did you not yourself tell me that one must return a treasure that one has been keeping to its rightful owner? Well, the rightful owner has come, and He has reclaimed His treasure."

At that, Rabbi Me-ir quoted the words of Job (1:21): "The Lord has given, and the Lord has taken away; praised be the name of the Lord."

Midrash Mishlé, ch. 31,
ed. S. Buber, pp. 54b–55a

Heavenly Assizes

Rabha taught:

When, after his death, a man is led before the judgment seat of God, he will be asked the following questions:

Did you conduct your business affairs with integrity?

Did you set aside fixed times for the study of the Torah?

Did you fulfill the commandment of procreation?

Did you hope for salvation?

Did you occupy yourself dialectically with wisdom?

Did you learn to understand how one thing follows from another?

B. *Shabbath* 31a

Rabbi Hezekiah and Rabbi Cohen both taught in the name of Rabh:

In the eschatological future, a man will have to give an account concerning everything in which his eye delighted, but the enjoyment of which he nevertheless denied himself.

P. *Qiddushin* IV, 12, ed. Krotoshin, p. 66d.

· IV ·
ABOUT REVELATION
AND TORAH

In the Beginning Was Wisdom

Rabbi Osha'ya began his sermon with the elucidation of the following verses:

> *Does not Wisdom call,*
> *does not understanding raise her voice? . . .*
> *The Lord created me as the beginning of His way,*
> *as the first of His acts of old. . . .*
> *Then was I beside Him like a master workman;*
> *and I was daily His delight,*
> *rejoicing before Him always.*
> (Proverbs 8:1, 22, 30)

Since Wisdom is identical with Torah, those verses lend themselves to this understanding:

The Torah says of itself that it was the instrument of the Holy One, praised be He.

If an earthly king builds himself a palace, he usually does not build it with his own skill, but he employs an architect. But the architect, too, does not build on the basis of a sudden brainwave. Instead, he first uses plans and diagrams to determine where to place the rooms, and where to place the wicket doors.

So, too, the Holy One, praised be He, first looked into the Torah, and only then did He create the world. That is why the Torah says (Genesis 1:1): "In the (*or:* With the) Beginning, God created heaven and earth." "Beginning" refers to the Torah, of which it is said in Proverbs 8:22: "The Lord created me as the beginning of His way."

Genesis 1:1 must, therefore, be understood as follows: "With the Torah, God created heaven and earth."

> *Genesis Rabbah* I, 1, ed. Theodor-Albeck,
> pp. 1–2; cf. John 1:1–3

Creation and Revelation

Rabbi Simeon ben Laqish taught:

In the Hebrew original of the Creation story in Genesis, chapter one, it is written in connection with the creation on every day: "And there was evening and there was morning, *a* first day," and "*a* second day," and "*a* third day," and so forth. But after the creation on the sixth day, it is written (Genesis 1:31): "And there was evening and there was morning, *the* sixth day."

What is the special significance of the sixth day?

It is in order to draw your attention to the sixth day of the month of Siwan, the day on which Israel was to receive the Torah at Mount Sinai.

This teaches us that the Holy One, praised be He, entered into a conditional agreement with the works of Creation:

"If the Israelites accept the Torah, then you will continue to exist. But if the Israelites do not accept the Torah, then I shall cause you to revert to primordial chaos."

> B. *Shabbath* 88a

Only Israel Wanted the Torah

When the Holy One, praised be He, revealed Himself in order to give the Torah to Israel, it was not to Israel alone that He meant to give it, but He also offered it to all the other peoples.

First He went to the sons of Esau and asked them: "Are you willing to accept the Torah?"
They said to Him: "What is written in it?"
He replied: "You shall not murder!" (Exodus 20:13).
But the sons of Esau said: "Sovereign of the Universe, surely it was the very nature of our ancestor to be a murderer, as it is written: 'The hands are the hands of Esau' (Genesis 27:22). And it is written: 'By your sword you shall live' (Genesis 27:40). We cannot accept the Torah."

God then went to the Ammonites and the Moabites and asked them: "Are you willing to accept the Torah?"
They said to Him: "What is written in it?"
He replied: "You shall not commit adultery!" (Exodus 20:13).
But the Ammonites and the Moabites said: "Sovereign of the Universe, surely it is our very nature that we are the offspring of an immoral sexual union, as it is said: 'Thus the two daughters of Lot came to be with child by their father' (Genesis 19:36). We cannot accept the Torah."

God then went to the Ishmaelites and asked them: "Are you willing to accept the Torah?"
They said to Him: "What is written in it?"
He replied: "You shall not steal!" (Exodus 20:13).
But the Ishmaelites said: "Sovereign of the Universe, surely it was the very nature of our ancestor to be a robber, as it is said: 'He shall be a wild ass of a man; his hand against everyone, and everyone's hand against him' (Genesis 16:12). We cannot accept the Torah."

Thus did the Holy One, praised be He, go from people to people, offering them the Torah. But no people was willing to accept it.

At last He came to the Israelites. Without asking Him what was written in the Torah, the Israelites immediately responded: "All that the Lord has spoken we will do and we will learn to understand" (Exodus 24:7).

Siphré ad Deuteronomium, pisqa 343,
ed. Finkelstein, pp. 395–97; cf.
Pesiqta Rabbathi 21, ed. Friedmann, p. 99b

Like an Inverted Barrel

Moses led the people out of the camp toward God,
and they took their place at the foot
of the mountain.

(Exodus 19:17)

Note: The last six words of this sentence may, in the original Hebrew, also be understood as *"under the mountain."*

Rabbi Abdimi bar Ḥama bar Ḥassa said:
This teaches us that the Holy One, praised be He, lifted up the mountain over the Israelites, holding it like an inverted barrel. He said to them: "If you accept the Torah, well and good. If not, then this will be your burial place."

About this, Rabh Aḥa bar Jacob offered the following comment:
"If this had really been so, one could protest against the Torah. After all, the Israelites had to accept it under compulsion."

"Not so," replied Rabha. "In the days of King Ahasuerus, they accepted the Torah once more; but this time voluntarily. That is why it is said in Esther 9:27: 'The Jews undertook and irrevocably obligated themselves.' This means: the Jews now voluntarily undertook that to which they had long before obligated themselves."

B. *Shabbath* 88a

The Lethal and Reviving Word

Rabbi Azariah and Rabbi Aḥa said in the name of Rabbi Yoḥanan:

When the Israelites heard the first word of the Ten Commandments at Mount Sinai, their souls left them.

The word returned to the Holy One, praised be He, and said: "Sovereign of the Universe, You live eternally, and Your Torah lives eternally. But You have sent me to the dead. They are all dead!"

Thereupon God made the word more palatable.

Rabbi Simeon bar Yoḥai taught:

The Torah, which the Holy One, praised be He, then gave to Israel, restored their souls to them. That is why it is said in Psalm 19:8: "The Torah of the Lord is perfect, restoring the soul."

Canticles Rabbah V, 16, iii

Everyone According to His Ability

Rabbi Yoḥanan said:

When the Voice of God came forth at Mount Sinai, it divided itself into the seventy languages of humankind, so that all peoples would be able to understand it.

Rabbi Tanḥuma said:

The Voice of God at Mount Sinai was understood by everyone according to his ability to understand. The old people understood it according to their ability. The young people understood it according to their ability, and similarly the children, the infants and the women.

Even Moses himself understood only in accordance with his own ability. That is why it is said in Exodus 19:19: "As Moses

spoke, God answered him with a voice." This means: with a voice
that Moses was able to bear.

Exodus Rabbah V, 9; cf.
Midrash Tanḥuma, Shemoth, 25

Bring Your Own Tablets

The disciples asked Rabbi Yoḥanan ben Zakkai:
"Why are the first tablets of the Ten Commandments said to
have been the work of God Himself (Exodus 32:16), whereas,
when Moses had shattered those tablets upon seeing the Golden
Calf (Exodus 32:19), the second set of tablets is described as having
been carved out of stone by Moses himself (Exodus 34:1)?"
Rabbi Yoḥanan answered this question with a parable:

This can be compared to a king who married a woman. He
employed the scribe and supplied him with his own paper for the
marriage document. And from his own possessions, he presented
the bride with a nuptial diadem. Then the king brought his bride
into his house.

Later, the king saw that his wife was sporting with one of the
manservants. The king became enraged, and he threw her out of
his house.

Now the bride's agent came before the king and said: "Your
Majesty, do you not know whence you have got yourself this
woman? Was it not from among the slaves? Because she grew up
among the slaves, she behaves arrogantly and learns from them."

The king replied: "What, then, would you have me do? Perchance that I get reconciled to her? In that case, bring your own
paper and your own scribe to get a new marriage document written, and I shall add my signature."

Moses, too, spoke in this manner to the Holy One, praised be
He, after Israel had worshiped the Golden Calf. He said: "Do You
not know whence You have got Yourself this people? Was it not
from Egypt, a place of idolatry?"

The Holy One, praised be He, replied: "What, then, would you have Me do? Perchance that I get reconciled to Israel? In that case, bring your own tablets, and I shall add My signature!"

Deuteronomy Rabbah, 'Eqebh, 17, ed. Liebermann, p. 91;
cf. *Tosephta Baba Qamma* 7:4,
ed. Zuckermandel, pp. 357f.

Honoring Father and Mother

They asked Rabbi Eli'ezer: "How far does one have to go in fulfilling the commandment about honoring one's father and one's mother?"

He replied: "Why do you ask me? You should be asking Dama ben Nethina!"

Dama ben Nethina, a pagan, was head of the city council of Ashkelon. One day, his mother hit him with a shoe in the presence of the whole council. The shoe dropped out of her hand. But Dama picked up the shoe and returned it to his mother, to save her the trouble of bending down.

Dama also never sat upon the stone on which his father used to sit. When his father died, he revered that stone as an object of worship.

It once happened that the jasper of the high priest's breastplate (cf. Exodus 28:15–21) was lost. The jasper represented the tribe of Benjamin. Inquiries were made to locate someone who owned a jasper; and it was learned that Dama ben Nethina was the owner of such a precious stone.

The Sages of Israel went to Dama ben Nethina, and they reached an agreement with him that they would buy the jasper from him for one hundred denarii. But when Dama wanted to bring the stone, he discovered that his father was sleeping on the little chest in which the jasper was kept; and Dama refused to wake up his father on that account.

The Sages now offered him one thousand denarii; but Dama did not wake his father.

Later, when the father awoke, Dama brought the stone to the Sages. They wanted to pay him the price of one thousand denarii, which they had last offered him. But he said to them: "How could I sell you the honor that I owe my father?" Instead, he sold them the jasper for the price upon which they had first agreed, one hundred denarii.

How did God reward him for this?

Rabbi Yossé bar Abun related that, on that very night, Dama's cow gave birth to a red calf. Once, when the Israelites were in need of a red heifer for the purification ritual (cf. Numbers 19:1–22), they bought that red heifer from Dama and paid him its weight in gold.

P. *Pe-ah* I, 1, ed. Krotoshin, p. 15c; cf. b. *Qiddushin* 31a

The Unwitting Fulfillment of a Commandment

Biblical law ordains that, at harvest time, any forgotten sheaves of grain on the field may not be gathered in by the farmer. They are considered to be the property of the poor and the strangers. See Leviticus 19:9–10; and cf. Ruth, ch. 2.

It once happened that a pious man forgot a measure of wheat on his field.

He said to his son: "Go and sacrifice a bull as a burnt offering, and another bull as a peace offering on my behalf!"

The son asked him: "But, Father, why are you happier about the commandment concerning the forgotten sheaves of grain than you are about all the other commandments that are stated in the Torah?"

The father replied: "The All-Present One gave us all the other commandments of the Torah, so that we obey them intentionally. But this is a commandment that we can only fulfill unwittingly. For, if we had intentionally left that measure of wheat on the field, we would have been unable to observe this particular command-ment."

Tosephta Pe-ah 3:18, ed. Lieberman, p. 53

Words of the Living God

A debate between the Schools of Shammai and Hillel had lasted for three years. These insisted that the law be decided according to their opinion, and those insisted that the law be decided according to their opinion.

Finally a Heavenly Voice was heard: "The opinion of these and the opinion of those are both the words of the Living God! But the law should be decided according to the opinion of the School of Hillel!"

But how could that have been? Since both opinions were the "words of the Living God," what gave the School of Hillel the right to decide the law only in accordance with their opinion?

It happened because the Sages of the School of Hillel were friendly and modest. They studied not only their own traditions, but also those of the School of Shammai. Indeed, they transmitted the teachings of the School of Shammai even before they transmitted their own teachings.

B. *'Erubhin* 13b

Divine Word, Human Interpretations

Abbaye said:
When it says in Psalm 62:12:

> *One thing God has spoken;*
> *two things have I heard:*
> *that might belongs to God,*

it means that one Scripture verse is open to several different interpretations, and that one and the same teaching must not be derived from several Scripture verses.

In the School of Rabbi Ishmael, they cited Jeremiah 23:29:

> *Is not My word like fire,*
> *says the Lord,*
> *and like a hammer that smites the rock?*

What happens when a hammer smites the rock?
Sparks fly.
Every single spark is the result of the impact of the hammer upon the rock. But no single spark is the sole result.

Thus, too, one single Scripture verse can transmit many different teachings.

B. *Sanhedrin* 34a; cf. b. *Shabbath* 88b

God Smiled

The Rabbis had been arguing about a certain point in the law of levitical purity and impurity. Rabbi Eli'ezer had brought forward all possible arguments in support of his position—without being able to convince his colleagues.

Then Rabbi Eli'ezer said: "Even this carob tree can prove that the law must be construed in the way I have argued!"

And the carob tree uprooted itself and moved one hundred cubits away. Some even insist that it moved four hundred cubits away.

But the other Rabbis said: "A carob tree cannot serve as proof."

Rabbi Eli'ezer said: "If the law is to be construed in the way I have argued, then let the stream of water here prove it!"

And the stream of water began to flow backward.

But the other Rabbis said: "A stream of water cannot serve as proof."

Again, Rabbi Eli'ezer said: "If the law is to be construed in the way I have argued, then let the walls of this House of Study prove it!"

And the walls of the House of Study began to incline.

But Rabbi Joshua rebuked them and said: "What business is it of yours, you walls, if the scholars have a disagreement about a point of law!"

The walls did not, therefore, fall down completely—out of respect for Rabbi Joshua. But, out of respect for Rabbi Eli'ezer, they also did not straighten up completely again. They remained standing in an inclining position.

Rabbi Eli'ezer now cried out: "If the law is to be construed in the way I have argued, then let God Himself prove it!"

And, in fact, a Heavenly Voice was heard proclaiming: "What do you want from Rabbi Eli'ezer? Don't you know that in all matters of law the decision is in accordance with his opinion?"

At that, Rabbi Joshua jumped to his feet and shouted: "It is not in the heavens!" (Deuteronomy 30:12).

What did he mean by that quotation from Deuteronomy?

Rabbi Jeremiah explained: "The Torah had already been revealed at Mount Sinai. We, therefore, need not be concerned with further Heavenly Voices. After all, the Sinaitic Torah itself contains the principle that, in legal matters, the vote of the majority is decisive" (Exodus 23:2, in the rabbinic interpretation).

Later, when Rabbi Nathan met the Prophet Elijah, he asked the Prophet: "What did the Holy One, praised be He, do at that hour?"

Elijah replied: "He smiled and said: 'My children have prevailed against Me! My children have prevailed against Me!' "

B. *Baba Mezi'a* 59b

The Fox and the Fishes

Our Masters taught:

The wicked Roman government once forbade the Jews to study the Torah and to live according to its provisions.

But Pappus ben Judah saw that Rabbi 'Aqiba had convened a public gathering for the purpose of Torah study.

Pappus said to him: "'Aqiba, are you not afraid of the government?"

'Aqiba replied: "I shall explain the situation to you by means of a parable:

"One day, a fox was strolling along by the banks of a river. He saw how the fishes were anxiously swimming around from place to place. He asked them: 'From what are you trying to escape?'

"The fishes answered: 'From the nets that people have cast for us.'

"The fox said: 'Why do you not come up and find safety on land, so that you and I can live together in peace, just as my ancestors have done with your ancestors in the past?'

"But the fishes replied: 'Are you really the one whom they call the most clever among the animals? You are not clever at all, but quite dumb. If we are already afraid in the element in which we live, how much more would we have to be afraid in the element in which we are certainly going to die!'

"And thus," Rabbi 'Aqiba continued, "is the matter with us. If we are already in a dangerous situation when we sit and study the Torah, of which it is said: 'For thereby you shall have life and shall long endure' (Deuteronomy 30:20), how much more dangerous would our situation be were we to neglect the Torah!"

B. *Berakhoth* 61b

"This Is the Torah, and That Is Its Reward!"

Rabh Judah taught in the name of Rabh:

When Moses ascended above, he found the Holy One, praised be He, occupied in attaching little crowns to the letters of the Torah.

Moses asked Him: "Sovereign of the Universe, why is that necessary?"

He answered: "At the end of many generations, a man will arise, 'Aqiba ben Joseph by name, who, on the basis of every little tittle, will expound heaps and heaps of legal teachings."

"Sovereign of the Universe," Moses requested, "please, let me see him."

"Turn around," said God.

Moses now went to 'Aqiba's academy and, out of modesty, sat down behind the eighth row of 'Aqiba's disciples, in order to listen to the lecture. But he was unable to follow the arguments, and he did not feel well.

However, when a certain subject was broached, the disciples asked their Master: "Whence do you know this?" And 'Aqiba replied: "This is a law that was given to Moses on Mount Sinai."

Hearing this, Moses began to feel better.

Moses returned to the Holy One, praised be He, and said to

Him: "Sovereign of the Universe, You have such a man at Your disposal; yet You are giving the Torah through me!"

"Be quiet!" God replied. "Such is My decree!"

Then Moses said: "Sovereign of the Universe, You have shown me his Torah. Now show me his reward."

"Turn around," said God.

Moses turned around and saw how—after 'Aqiba's martyrdom—they were weighing out his flesh in the market stalls.

"Sovereign of the Universe," Moses cried out, "this is the Torah, and that is its reward!"

"Be quiet!" God replied. "Such is My decree!"

B. *Menaḥoth* 29b

No Excuse

Our Masters taught:

A poor man, a rich man and a sensual man come before the Heavenly Tribunal.

The poor man is asked: "Why did you not occupy yourself with the Torah?"

If he answers: "I was poor and concerned about my livelihood," he will be asked: "Do you mean to say that you were poorer than Hillel?"

For it is told of Hillel the Elder that he daily went to work, in order to earn half a denarius. Half of it he would give to the watchman at the House of Study to gain permission to enter the House of Study, and the other half he would spend on his needs and the needs of his household.

One day he was unable to earn anything, and the watchman did not let him enter the House of Study. So he climbed on the roof and sat upon an opening in order to hear the words of the Living God out of the mouth of Shemaya and Abhtalyon. They say that this happened on a Friday during the winter, and that snow fell upon him.

At dawn, Shemaya said to Abhtalyon: "Abhtalyon, my brother, every day this house is light, but today it is dark. Is it perhaps a cloudy day?"

They looked up, and saw the figure of a man in the roof's opening. They went up and found Hillel, who was covered by three cubits of snow. They brought him down, bathed him and rubbed him with oil. Then they sat him down in front of the fire, saying: "This man is worthy of having the Sabbath desecrated for his sake."

The rich man is asked: "Why did you not occupy yourself with the Torah?"

If he answers: "I was rich and concerned about my wealth," he will be asked: "Do you mean to say that you were richer than Rabbi Ele'azar?"

For it is told of Rabbi Ele'azar ben Harsom that his father left him an inheritance of one thousand hamlets on land and, correspondingly, one thousand ships on the sea. Nevertheless, he daily took a bag of flour upon his shoulder and wandered from city to city—for the sole purpose of studying the Torah. He never did see the hamlets that his father had left him, for he sat studying the Torah day and night.

The sensual man is asked: "Why did you not occupy yourself with the Torah?"

If he answers: "I was so good-looking and had so much to do just keeping my passion under control," he will be asked: "Do you mean to say that you were better-looking than Joseph?"

For it is told about Joseph the Righteous that Potiphar's wife daily attempted to seduce him with words. The dresses she put on for him in the morning she no longer wore in the evening. The dresses she put on for him in the evening she no longer wore the next morning.

She said to him: "Obey me!"

But he answered: "No!"

She said to him: "I shall have you put in jail."

He answered: "The Lord sets prisoners free" (Psalm 146:7).

She said to him: "I shall bend your high stature."

He answered: "The Lord makes those who are bent stand straight" (Psalm 146:8).

She said to him: "I shall have your eyes blinded."

He answered: "The Lord restores sight to the blind" (Psalm 146:8).

Then she offered him one thousand pieces of silver, if only he would obey her, "to lie beside her, to be with her" (Genesis 39:10).

But he would not obey her. He neither wanted "to lie beside her" in this world, nor did he have any desire "to be with her" in the next.

Thus the poor who do not study Torah stand condemned by the example set by Hillel. The rich who do not study Torah stand condemned by the example set by Rabbi Ele'azar ben Harsom. And the sensual who do not study Torah stand condemned by the example that Joseph had set.

B. *Yoma* 35b

For the Sake of Peace

Rabbi Simeon ben Laqish said:

Great is peace, for, in order to make peace between Joseph and his brothers, Scripture uses some fictitious words.

When their father had died, the brothers were afraid that Joseph would now wreak vengeance on them. That is why they said to him: "Before his death, your father left this instruction: So shall you say to Joseph, 'Forgive, I urge you, the offense and guilt of your brothers who treated you so harshly' " (Genesis 50:16f.).

However, nowhere in Scripture do we find that our Father Jacob had actually given such an instruction. Scripture uses some fictitious words here—for the sake of peace.

Deuteronomy Rabbah, Shophetim, 15,
ed. Liebermann, p. 102

The Guardians of the City

Once upon a time, Rabbi Judan Nesiah sent out Rabbi Ḥiyya, Rabbi Assi and Rabbi Ammi. They were to visit all the cities in the Land of Israel and to see to the appointment of teachers of Scripture and teachers of *Mishnah* (i.e., the "Oral Torah").

They came to a city in which no teacher was to be found. They then ordered: "Let the guardians of the city appear before us!"

A detachment of the local militia was brought before them.

"But these are not the guardians of the city!" the Rabbis said. "These are the destroyers of the city!"

The local inhabitants now wanted to know: "Who, then, in your opinion, *are* the guardians of the city!"

The Rabbis replied: "The guardians of the city are the teachers of Scripture and the teachers of *Mishnah*. That is why it is said in Psalm 127:1: 'Unless the Lord watches over the city, the watchman keeps vigil in vain.' "

P. *Ḥagigah* I, 7, ed. Krotoshin, p. 76c

No "Old" Testament

Take to heart these words
with which I charge you today.
(Deuteronomy 6:6)

"With which I charge you *today.*" They are not to be in your sight like some old ordinance, to which nobody is paying attention any longer. But they are to be in your sight like a new ordinance, toward which everybody is running.

Siphré ad Deuteronomium, pisqa 33,
ed. Finkelstein, p. 59

· V ·
ABOUT THE
GREATEST
COMMANDMENT

This Is the Whole Torah

A non-Jew once came to Shammai and said to him: "Convert me to Judaism, on condition that you can teach me the whole Torah while I am standing on one foot."

With a builder's measuring rod in his hand, Shammai angrily threw him out.

The non-Jew then went to Hillel and repeated his request: "Convert me to Judaism, on condition that you can teach me the whole Torah while I am standing on one foot."

Hillel converted him and taught him as follows: "What is hateful to you, do not do to your neighbor. This is the whole Torah. All the rest is commentary. Go now and study it!"

B. *Shabbath* 31a

Still a Greater One

Love your neighbor as yourself.
(Leviticus 19:18)

Rabbi 'Aqiba said: "This is the great principle of the Torah."

But Ben 'Azzai said: "There is an even greater one than this. It is found in Genesis 5:1: 'This is the book of the generations of Man. When God created Man, He made him in the likeness of God.' (For here, not only the neighbor is involved, but all human beings.)"

Siphra, Qedoshim, pereq 4:12, ed. Weiss, p. 89b

From Moses to Habakkuk

Rabbi Simlai preached:
Six hundred and thirteen commandments were revealed through Moses.
Then David came, and found their basis in eleven commandments, as it is said in the fifteenth Psalm:

    A psalm of David.
    Lord, who may stay in Your tent,
      who may reside on Your holy mountain?
  (i)   He who lives without blame,
  (ii)   who does what is right,
  (iii)   and in his heart acknowledges the truth;
  (iv)   who has no slander upon his tongue;
  (v)   who has never done harm to his fellow,
  (vi)   or borne reproach for his acts toward his neighbor;
  (vii) for whom a contemptible man is abhorrent,
 (viii) but who honors those who fear the Lord;

   (ix)   who stands by his oath even to his hurt;
   (x)   who has never lent money on interest,
   (xi)   or accepted a bribe against the innocent.
          The man who acts thus shall never be shaken.

Then Isaiah came, and found the basis in six commandments, as it is said in Isaiah 35:15–16:

   (i)   He who walks in righteousness,
   (ii)   speaks uprightly,
   (iii)   spurns profit from fraudulent dealings,
   (iv)   waves away a bribe instead of grasping it,
   (v)   stops his ears against listening to infamy,
   (vi)   shuts his eyes against looking at evil—
        such a one shall dwell in lofty security.

Then Micah came, and found the basis in three commandments, as it is said in Micah 6:8:

        He has told you, O man, what is good,
        and what the Lord requires of you:
   (i)   Only to do justice
   (ii)   and to love goodness,
   (iii)   and to walk humbly with your God.

Then Isaiah returned, and found the basis in two commandments, as it is said in Isaiah 56:1:

        Thus said the Lord:
   (i)   Observe what is right
   (ii)   and do what is just.

Then Amos came, and found the basis in one single commandment, as it is said in Amos 5:4:

        Thus said the Lord to the House of Israel:
   (i)   Seek Me, and you will live!

But Rabh Nahman bar Isaac objected to this: "Amos 5:4 could

be understood to imply that God is to be sought through the observance of the entire Torah (which would give us a basis of six hundred and thirteen commandments, and not the single commandment that is the basis of them all). Rather would we have to say that the Prophet who found the basis of all the commandments in one single commandment was Habakkuk, who (in Habakkuk 2:4) said: 'The righteous shall live by his faith.' "

B. *Makkoth* 23b, 24a

The Brief Text

Bar Qappara explained:

What is the brief text upon which all the major parts of the Torah depend?

It is Proverbs 3:6:

> *In all your ways acknowledge Him,*
> *and He will make straight your paths.*

B. *Berakhoth* 63a

· VI ·
ABOUT THE TEACHERS
OF TORAH

Rabbi 'Aqiba Laughed

Rabbah bar Bar Ḥanah taught:
When Rabbi Eli'ezer took sick, his disciples visited him.
He said to them: "God must be very angry with me."
They all cried; but Rabbi 'Aqiba laughed.
"Why do you laugh?" they asked him.
"And why do you cry?" he asked in return.
They replied: "Why should we not cry when the Scroll of the
Torah (as they reverently called Rabbi Eli'ezer) lies in pain here?"
Rabbi 'Aqiba retorted: "It is precisely for this reason that I am
laughing. As long as I saw that the Master's wine never turned
sour, that his flax was never destroyed, that his oil never putrefied
and that his honey never became rancid, I thought that, God
forbid, he might already have received all of his reward in this
world. But now that I see him lying in pain, I am happy because
I know that his reward is awaiting him in the World-to-Come."

Rabbi Eli'ezer himself now joined the conversation, and he
asked: " 'Aqiba, do you mean to imply that I am suffering because
I have neglected a single part of the whole Torah?"
'Aqiba answered: "Master, you yourself have taught us the
Scripture verse: 'Surely there is not a righteous man on earth who
only does good and never sins!' " (Ecclesiastes 7:20).
B. Sanhedrin 101a

Unprepared in Synagogue

God spoke all these words, saying.
(Exodus 20:1)

Why, in this introduction to the Ten Commandments, does Scripture use *two* words: *spoke* and *saying?*

This can be explained by means of the following verses from the Book of Job.

First it says:

> *Then He saw it [Wisdom], and declared it;*
> *He prepared it, and He probed it.*
> (Job 28:27)

And only *then* does it state:

> *And He said to man.*
> (Job 28:28)

The Torah teaches you that, if you are a Torah scholar, you must not be so haughty as to tell the congregation something that you have not previously clarified for yourself two or three times.

It once happened that, at a public worship service, the synagogue official called upon Rabbi 'Aqiba to read from the Torah. But he refused to go up to the reading desk.

Then his disciples said to him: "Master, have you not taught us yourself that the Torah is our life and the length of our days? Why, then, do you refuse to go up to the reading desk?"

Rabbi 'Aqiba answered: "By the Temple cult! I only refuse to read from the Torah in public because I have not previously gone over today's pericope two or three times, in preparation for the reading. It is not permitted to recite something before the assembled congregation unless one has previously clarified it for oneself two or three times. We find this to be the case also with the Holy One, praised be He, Himself. He who gave man the power of speech, and for whom the Torah is as clear and lucid as a bright star, even He, as it is written, before giving the Torah to Israel, first 'saw it, and declared it, prepared it, and probed it,' and only afterward 'He said (it) to man.' That also is the reason why, in Exodus 20:1, it says: 'God spoke all these words,' meaning that He spoke them to Himself; and only afterward 'saying,' that is, saying them to the Israelites."

Midrash Tanḥuma, Yithro, 15

With All Your Soul

Rabbi 'Aqiba had disobeyed Hadrian's prohibition of teaching the Torah. See page 44, "The Fox and the Fishes." He was arrested and condemned to die a cruel martyr's death.

When he was tortured in the presence of the wicked Roman governor Tinneius Rufus, the time came for the "Hear, O Israel!" (beginning with Deuteronomy 6:4–9) to be recited. 'Aqiba recited it and smiled.

The Roman official shouted at him: "Old man, how can you smile in your pain? You are either a magician, or you make fun of your sufferings."

'Aqiba answered: "I am no magician, and I do not make fun of my sufferings. But throughout all my life I have recited the words 'You must love the Lord your God with all your heart and with all your soul and with all your might' (Deuteronomy 6:5), and I was sad when I could not understand how I might possibly love God with all my soul. I have loved God with all my heart and with all my might. But it was never clear to me how I could also love Him with all my soul. Now that I am giving up my soul, and the hour of the 'Hear, O Israel!' has come, while I am determined to remain true to my resolve, should I not be smiling?"

As he spoke thus, his soul left him.

P. *Berakhoth* IX, 7, ed. Krotoshin, p. 14b

Authority

When the Jewish calendar was still calculated on the basis of an actual sighting of the new moon each month, Rabbi Joshua and Rabban Gamaliel II, president of the Supreme Court, once had a disagreement about the actual beginning of the month of Tishri. That is the month during which the Jewish High Holy Days—New Year and the Day of Atonement—occur. Each Rabbi insisted upon his own lunar calculation. But, when all was said and done, Rabban Gamaliel was the one invested with supreme authority.

Rabban Gamaliel now addressed the following command to Rabbi Joshua: "I order you to appear before me on the day that, according to your calculation, is the Day of Atonement; and you are to bring with you your staff and your purse (the carrying of which on the Day of Atonement is prohibited)!"

Rabbi 'Aqiba went to see Rabbi Joshua and found him in a state of great sadness.

'Aqiba said to him: "I can prove to you that what Rabban Gamaliel has done is valid. Leviticus 23:4 says: '*These* are the festivals of the Lord, the sacred occasions, which *you* shall proclaim each at its appointed time.' It is as though God were saying: 'Whether at the right time or at the wrong time, I know of no other festivals than *these.*'"

When Rabbi Joshua went to see Rabbi Dossa ben Harkinas, the latter said to him: "If we were to review critically the decisions of Rabban Gamaliel's court, we would also be obligated to review critically the decisions of every single court of law that had been appointed from the days of Moses until today."

On the day that, according to his own calculation, was the Day of Atonement, Rabbi Joshua took his staff and his money and went to Rabban Gamaliel in Jamnia.

Rabban Gamaliel arose and kissed Rabbi Joshua on his head. Then he said to him: "Come in peace, my Master and my disciple! My Master, in wisdom; my disciple, because you have obeyed my command."

Mishnah Rosh Hashanah 2:9

Strength of Character

'Aqabya ben Mahalaleel testified to four traditions before the assembly of his colleagues.

They said to him: " 'Aqabya, renounce those four traditions that you have recited before us, and we shall appoint you vice president of the Supreme Court of all Israel!"

But 'Aqabya replied: "It would be better for me to be called a fool all my life than to be considered wicked by God for even an hour. It shall not be said of me that I have renounced the traditions to which I have testified for the sake of high office." . . .

In the hour of his death, he said to his son: "My son, renounce the four traditions that I have taught!"

But his son said to him: "Then why did you not renounce them yourself?"

The father replied: "I have heard them from the mouth of a majority; and my opponents heard their traditions, too, from the mouth of a majority. That is why I remained faithful to what I had heard, and they remained faithful to what they had heard. But you have heard those traditions from the mouth of an individual only, and you have heard the opposite from the mouth of a majority. It is, therefore, better for you to forsake the opinion of an individual and to accept the opinion of the majority, instead."

The son now asked his father: "Father, recommend me to your colleagues."

'Aqabya replied: "I shall not recommend you."

"But why not? Have you, perhaps, found anything wrong with me?"

"Certainly not! But it is your own deeds that will have to bring you close to them, and your own deeds that might remove you from them."

Mishnah 'Eduyoth 5:6–7

Rebellion at the Academy

Our Masters taught:

A disciple once came to Rabbi Joshua and asked: "Is the evening prayer an obligatory prayer or a voluntary prayer?"

Rabbi Joshua answered: "It is a voluntary prayer."

The disciple then went to Rabban Gamaliel II and asked him the same question: "Is the evening prayer an obligatory prayer or is it a voluntary prayer?"

Rabban Gamaliel answered: "It is an obligatory prayer."

The disciple then said: "But Rabbi Joshua considers it to be a voluntary prayer!"

"Wait," replied Rabban Gamaliel, "until the scholars assemble in the House of Study."

When the scholars were all gathered in the House of Study, someone raised the question: "Is the evening prayer an obligatory prayer or is it a voluntary prayer?"

Rabban Gamaliel answered: "It is an obligatory prayer."

Then he turned to the scholars and asked: "Is there anyone here who would contradict this ruling?"

Rabbi Joshua answered: "No."

Rabban Gamaliel turned to Rabbi Joshua and said: "But have I not been told that you consider the evening prayer to be a voluntary prayer? Stand up, and let the witness testify against you!"

Rabbi Joshua stood up and said: "If I were alive, and the witness dead, the living could contradict the dead. But, seeing that I am alive and the witness is alive, how could the living contradict the living?"

Rabban Gamaliel remained seated and delivered his discourse. But Rabbi Joshua had to remain standing—until the scholars began to shout and to command Huzpith to stop. He stopped. (Huzpith was the assistant who clarified Gamaliel's discourse to the students.)

Then the scholars said: "How long are we going to tolerate Rabban Gamaliel's insulting Rabbi Joshua? Last year, he insulted him in connection with the matter of the New Year calculation. (See page 58, "Authority.") Then he insulted him in connection with Rabbi Zadoq's firstling (cf. b. *Bekhoroth* 36a). And now he is insulting him again. Let us depose Rabban Gamaliel as head of the academy."

They did so.

But then they asked themselves: "Whom can we now appoint as head of the academy? We cannot appoint Rabbi Joshua, because he is involved in this matter. We cannot appoint Rabbi 'Aqiba, because Rabban Gamaliel could curse him on account of the fact that, being of nonscholarly origins, 'Aqiba has no ancestral merits to show for himself. The most suitable person would be Rabbi Ele'azar ben Azariah. He is wise, so that he is able to answer all questions put to him. He is wealthy, so that he is sufficiently respected by the Roman administration to be able to represent us. And he is a descendant of Ezra in the tenth generation, so that Rabban Gamaliel could not curse him on account of any nonscholarly origins."

They went to Rabbi Ele'azar and asked him whether they might appoint him as head of the academy.

Rabbi Ele'azar answered: "I must first discuss the matter with the members of my family."

He went and asked his wife.

She said to him: "But, perhaps, they will later depose you, too?"

He replied: "There is a proverb that says: 'Drink out of the goblet of honor, even if it gets broken tomorrow.' "

She said: "But you do not have any white hair to command the necessary respect!"

He was at that time eighteen years old. But a miracle happened, and eighteen rows of his hair turned white. He now looked like a man of seventy, and he accepted the position.

A reciter of traditions related:

On that day, they dismissed the doorkeeper, and they permitted all students to enter the House of Study. For Rabban Gamaliel, while in office, had decreed: "No student whose inside is not as clean as his outside may enter the House of Study!"

On that day, many new benches were brought into the House

of Study. Rabbi Yoḥanan reported that there was a difference of opinion between Abba Joseph ben Dosethai and the other Rabbis as to whether there were four hundred or seven hundred new benches.

Rabban Gamaliel now became concerned that, while he was head of the academy, he might, God forbid, have withheld the Torah from Israel. But, in a dream, he was shown white jugs filled with ashes—to assure him that he had indeed kept out of the academy only the unworthy students. Yet the dream had no real significance, and it was solely meant for the purpose of calming him down. (For Rabban Gamaliel had, in fact, prevented worthy students from studying.) . . .

On that day, many important decisions in matters of religious law were reached. Rabban Gamaliel did not absent himself from a single session; but, in the matters under discussion, the majority always sided with Rabbi Joshua.

Rabban Gamaliel realized that this was the case, and he decided to apologize to Rabbi Joshua.

When he came to Rabbi Joshua's house, he saw that the walls of the house were black. He said to Rabbi Joshua: "It can be recognized from the walls of your house that you are a blacksmith."

But Rabbi Joshua replied: "Woe unto the generation whom you serve as spiritual head! You seem to have no idea at all about the troubles of the scholars and about their struggle for their daily bread."

Rabban Gamaliel said to him: "I ask for your pardon. Forgive me."

But Rabbi Joshua did not respond.

Rabban Gamaliel then said: "Do it out of respect for my father." Then they became reconciled. . . .

The scholars now had a problem: "What shall we do? We cannot depose Rabbi Ele'azar, for we abide by the principle 'In holy things one ascends and does not descend.' If, on the other hand, we let the two Masters preach on alternate Sabbaths, this would lead to jealousy—for it would then not be clear who of the two is president of the Sanhedrin, and who is head of the academy. Let Rabban Gamaliel, therefore, preach on three successive Sabbaths, and let Rabbi Ele'azar ben Azariah preach on the following Sabbath!"

B. *Berakhoth* 27b, 28a; cf. p. *Berakhoth* IV, 1, ed. Krotoshin,
pp. 7c, d

The Earthen Vessel

(Rabbi Joshua ben Ḥananiah was very ugly.)

One day, the daughter of the Emperor said to Rabbi Joshua: "Such beautiful Torah in such an ugly vessel!"

He answered: "Learn the reason for this from your father's palace. Tell me, how do they keep the wine in your palace?"

"In earthen vessels," she replied.

Rabbi Joshua professed amazement: "In earthen vessels! That's what the common people do, who keep their wine in earthen vessels. You should be keeping your wine in golden or in silver vessels."

She went home, and had all the wine poured into golden and silver vessels.

The wine turned sour.

Later, Rabbi Joshua said to her: "This is the way in which it goes with the Torah, too."

"But are there not handsome people, who nevertheless are learned?" the Emperor's daughter wanted to know.

"Of course, there are!" replied Rabbi Joshua. "But they would even be more learned if they were less handsome."

B. *Nedarim* 50b; cf. b. *Ta'anith* 7a

Rabbi Joshua Defeated

Rabbi Joshua ben Ḥananiah related:

Nobody has ever defeated me—except for a woman, a little boy and a little girl.

What happened in the case of the woman?

I once stayed at an inn, and every day the hostess cooked beans for me. On the first day, I ate them all, without leaving any over. On the second day, I also did not leave any over. On the third day, she had cooked them with too much salt, and as soon as I had tasted the beans, I kept my hand away from them.

The hostess asked: "Master, why don't you eat?"

I replied: "I have already eaten earlier today."

"Then you should not have stretched out your hand for the bread," she said. And she continued: "Is it possible, Master, that you have left today's plate as a substitute for the other meals you have eaten here, from which you have left nothing by way of a gratuity for the waiters? For the Sages have taught that, while it is not permitted to leave anything in the pot, one must leave something on the plate."

What happened in the case of the little girl?

I was once on a journey, and there was a path that led through a field. I used that path. Then a little girl called out at me: "Master, is this not a part of the field?"

"No," I replied, "it is a trodden path."

"Robbers like you have made it into such," she said to me.

And what happened in the case of the little boy?

Once again I was on a journey, and I noticed a little boy who was sitting at the crossroads. I asked him: "Which road does one take into the city?"

He replied: "This road here is short but long. And that road there is long but short."

I took the road that he had described as "short but long." But when I approached the city, I saw that the city was surrounded by gardens and orchards, and that one could get to the city by detours only. I, therefore, backtracked to the crossroads. When I saw the little boy, I said to him: "My son, have you not told me that this road was short?"

"And have I not told you 'but long'?" he replied.

Then I kissed him on his head and exclaimed: "Happy are you, O Israel! For you all are wise—the young as well as the old."

B. *'Erubhin* 53b

What Is to Become of the Torah?

Our Masters taught:

After Rabbi Me-ir died, Rabbi Judah said to his disciples: "Do not let the disciples of Rabbi Me-ir come into my House of Study! For they do not come to study Torah, but only to overwhelm me in arguments with their quotations from the Tradition."

Nevertheless, Symmachus succeeded in gaining entrance into Rabbi Judah's House of Study and in participating in the discussions.

When Rabbi Judah saw him, he became angry, and he said to his disciples: "Have I not told you not to let the disciples of Rabbi Me-ir come in here? They are so argumentative!"

Then Rabbi Yossé said: "Were we to obey you, people would rightfully say: 'Me-ir is dead; Judah is angry; and Yossé is silent. What, then, is to become of the Torah?'"

B. *Nazir* 49a; cf. b. *Qiddushin* 52b

He Threw Away the Peel

Elisha ben Abhuyah was a great rabbinic scholar of the second century c.e. But he became a heretic, and his former colleagues thereafter referred to him as *Aḥer,* i.e., "the other one." Only his disciple, Rabbi Me-ir, without sharing his master's heresy, remained loyal to him until the end of his life.

Rabbah bar Rabh Shilah once met the Prophet Elijah. He asked the Prophet: "With what does the Holy One, praised be He, occupy Himself?"

Elijah answered: "He is teaching the traditions in the name of all of the Rabbis—with the exception of the traditions of Rabbi Me-ir, in whose name He does not teach anything."

Rabbah asked: "But why not?"

Elijah answered: "Because Rabbi Me-ir learned his traditions from the mouth of *Aḥer.*"

To which Rabbah retorted: "Why should he not have done so? Rabbi Me-ir found a pomegranate. He ate the inside, but threw away the peel."

And the Prophet Elijah said: "Now that you have interceded on Rabbi Me-ir's behalf, I can actually hear the Holy One, praised be He, saying: 'My son Me-ir says . . .'"

B. *Ḥagigah* 15b

The Cold Dishes

For the wedding banquet of his son, Rabbi Simeon ben Rabbi (Judah the Patriarch) invited all of the Rabbis—with the exception of Bar Qappara, whom he did not invite.

Bar Qappara went, and he wrote upon the door of Rabbi Simeon's house:

After a man's joy comes death.
What profit, then, does he have from his joy?

When Rabbi Simeon saw this graffito, he asked: "Who has done this to me? Whom have we forgotten to invite?"

He was told that it was Bar Qappara.

Rabbi Simeon said: "Tomorrow I am giving a banquet especially in his honor."

He prepared a banquet, and he invited all the Rabbis, including, of course, Bar Qappara.

When the guests arrived, and when the various courses of the dinner were brought in, Bar Qappara told three hundred fox parables as each dish was brought in. The guests listened with so much rapt attention that the dishes were left untouched and turned cold.

Rabbi Simeon asked his servants: "Why do the dishes remain untouched?"

They replied: "An old man is sitting there, who, when each course is brought in, tells three hundred fox parables—until the dishes turn cold and are no longer eaten."

Hearing this, Rabbi Simeon approached Bar Qappara and asked him: "Why don't you let my guests eat?"

Bar Qappara answered: "Of what concern are your guests to me? I only came here to prove to you that Solomon was right when he complained: 'What does a man gain by all his toil?'" (Ecclesiastes 1:3).

Leviticus Rabbah XXVIII, 2, ed. Margulies,
pp. 653–54; cf. *Ecclesiastes Rabbah* I, 3

Comfort

When the son of Rabban Yoḥanan ben Zakkai died, his disciples came to comfort him.

Rabbi Eli'ezer came in, sat down before him and said to him: "Master, may I say something to you?"

"Speak!" answered Rabban Yoḥanan.

Rabbi Eli'ezer spoke: "Adam had a son who died. But Adam allowed himself to be comforted about him. How do we know that Adam allowed himself to be comforted? Because it is said in Genesis 4:25: 'Adam knew his wife again.' You, too, should accept comfort!"

But Rabban Yoḥanan said: "Is it not enough for me that I bear my own pain, without your reminding me of Adam's pain?"

Then Rabbi Joshua came in and asked for permission to utter some words of comfort. When that permission was granted, he said: "Job had sons and daughters, and they all died on the same day. Nevertheless, Job allowed himself to be comforted about them. How do we know that Job allowed himself to be comforted? Because it says in Job 1:21: 'The Lord has given, and the Lord has taken away; blessed be the name of the Lord.' "

But Rabban Yoḥanan said: "Is it not enough for me that I bear my own pain, without your reminding me of Job's pain?"

Then Rabbi Yossé came in, sat down before him and asked for permission to utter some words of comfort. When that permission was granted, he said: "Aaron had two grown-up sons, and they both died on the same day. Nevertheless, Aaron allowed himself to be comforted, as it is said in Leviticus 10:3: 'And Aaron was silent,' where 'silence' can only mean that he accepted comfort. You, too, should accept comfort!"

But Rabban Yoḥanan replied: "Is it not enough for me that I bear my own pain, without your reminding me of Aaron's pain?"

Then Rabbi Simeon came in and asked for permission to utter

some words of comfort. When that permission was granted, he said: "King David had a son who died. Nevertheless, he allowed himself to be comforted. You, too, should accept comfort! How do we know that David allowed himself to be comforted? Because it is said in 2 Samuel 12:24: 'David consoled his wife Bathsheba; he went to her and lay with her. She bore a son and she named him Solomon.' Master, you, too, should accept comfort!"

But Rabban Yoḥanan said to him: "Is it not enough for me that I bear my own pain, without your reminding me of King David's pain?"

Then Rabbi Ele'azar ben 'Arakh came in, and Rabban Yoḥanan knew at once that he would not be able to withstand Rabbi Ele'azar's attempts to comfort him. . . .

Rabbi Ele'azar sat down before him and said: "I shall tell you a parable. A king once deposited something with a certain man. Every day that man would moan and cry: 'Woe is me! When, at last, am I going to be free of this great responsibility, so that I can live in peace?' You, Master, had a son. He studied the Torah, the Prophets and the Hagiographa, and he studied the legal and the narrative components of rabbinic lore. And he left this world without sin. You should find comfort in the fact that you were able to return that which had been entrusted to you without blemish."

Rabban Yoḥanan said to him: "Ele'azar, my son, you have comforted me in the way people should comfort one another."

Abhoth deRabbi Nathan, Version A, chapter XIV,
ed. Schechter, pp. 29b, 30a

The Encounter

Mar Sutra, the son of Rabh Naḥman, once went from Sikara to Maḥuza, while Rabha and Rabh Saphra were on their way to Sikara.

They met.

Mar Sutra thought that the two scholars had come toward him for the sole purpose of greeting him. He said to them: "Why did the Rabbis take the trouble to walk so far in order to greet me?"

Rabh Saphra replied: "We did not even know that the Master was on his way. Had we known, we would have taken much more trouble."

Now Rabha said to Rabh Saphra: "Why did you have to tell him that? You must have annoyed him with your remark."

Rabh Saphra replied: "If I had not told him, we would have deceived him."

"No," said Rabha. "He would only have deceived himself."

B. *Ḥullin* 94b

· VII ·
ABOUT PRAYER

Entreaty

Rabbi Simeon used to say:

Be careful in the proclamation of the "Hear, O Israel!" (Deuteronomy 6:4–9; 11:13–21; Numbers 15:37–41) and in your prayer. When you pray, do not make your prayer a routine matter, but a beseeching and an entreaty for mercy before the All-Present One; as it is said: "For He is gracious and compassionate, slow to anger, abounding in kindness, and renouncing punishment" (Joel 2:13). And be not wicked in your own esteem!

Mishnah Abhoth 2:13

Long and Short Prayers

Our Masters taught:

A disciple once conducted public worship in the presence of Rabbi Eli'ezer, and he prayed for a very long time.

The other disciples complained to Rabbi Eli'ezer, saying: "What a prayer elaborator this man is!"

71

But Rabbi Eli'ezer replied: "Has he really prayed longer than our Master Moses, of whom Deuteronomy 9:25 reports that he once prayed for forty days and forty nights?"

On another occasion, a disciple conducted public worship in the presence of Rabbi Eli'ezer, and the service was rather short.

The other disciples complained to Rabbi Eli'ezer, saying: "What a prayer abbreviator this man is!"

But Rabbi Eli'ezer replied: "Has he really offered a shorter prayer than our Master Moses, of whom Numbers 12:13 reports that he once offered a prayer of only five words, 'O God, pray heal her'?"

B. *Berakhoth* 34a

"Do Your Will in Heaven"

When, in times of need and danger, one is unable to muster the requisite concentration and devotion for the daily Prayer of the Eighteen Benedictions, a brief prayer may be substituted.

Rabbi Eli'ezer suggests the following version:

> *Do Your will in heaven above,*
> *and grant equanimity*
> *to those who revere You on earth below;*
> *and do what seems good in Your sight.*
> *You are praised, O Lord,*
> *who hears prayer.*

B. *Berakhoth* 29b

Looking Upward

It is written in Exodus 17:11: "Whenever Moses held up his hand, Israel prevailed; but whenever he let down his hand, Amalek prevailed."

But could the hands of Moses really advance the battle or hinder the battle?

No. It only means that the Israelites were victorious as long as they looked upward and subjected their hearts to their Father in heaven. When they failed to do so, they suffered defeat.

Similar is the case of the brazen serpent, of which it is written in Numbers 21:8: "If anyone who is bitten looks at it, he shall recover."

Was, then, the brazen serpent able to kill or to grant recovery?

No. It only means that the Israelites were healed as long as they looked upward and subjected their hearts to their Father in heaven. When they failed to do so, they pined away.

Mishnah Rosh Hashanah 3:8

The Father Who Gives Rain

Hanan the Hidden One was the son of the daughter of Honi the Circle-Drawer.

Whenever the world needed rain, the Rabbis would send the schoolchildren to Hanan.

They used to pull at the corners of his garment, and say: "Father, Father! Give us rain!"

And Hanan would pray: "Sovereign of the Universe, do it for the sake of the little children, who are unable to distinguish between the Father, who can give rain, and the father who cannot give rain."

And then the rain would always fall.
Why was he called Ḥanan the Hidden One?
Because, out of modesty, he would always hide.

B. *Ta'anith* 23b

Vain Prayer

If someone cries out about something that can no longer be reversed, then this is a vain prayer.

How are we to understand this?

If someone whose wife is pregnant were to say: "May it be God's will that my wife give birth to a male child," then this would be a vain prayer.

Or if someone, walking on his way, were to hear cries emanating from the direction of the city, and if he then were to pray: "May it be God's will that those be not the members of my own family," then this would be a vain prayer.

Mishnah Berakhoth 9:3

"Why Do You Cry Out to Me?"

When the Israelites, pursued by the Egyptians, stood at the shores of the Sea of Reeds, they, according to Exodus 14:11–12, murmured against Moses. And Moses prayed to God.

But the Lord said to Moses: "Why do you cry out to Me? Tell the Israelites to go forward!" (Exodus 14:15).

Rabbi Joshua said:

The Holy One, praised be He, said to Moses: "The only thing Israel has to do is to go forward."

Rabbi Eli'ezer said:

The Holy One, praised be He, said to Moses: "Moses, My children are in distress. The sea is keeping them back, and the enemy is pursuing them from behind. And all you can think of is to cry out to Me, and to make long prayers! Why do you cry out to Me?"

Mekhilta, Wayehi Beshallaḥ, ch. III,
ed. Horovitz-Rabin, p. 97

Concerns of the Moment

One day Rabha saw that Rabh Hamnuna was spending a long time in prayer.

Rabha said: "Those people are neglecting eternal life (i.e., the study of the Torah, which leads to life eternal) and, instead, busy themselves with the concerns of the moment!"

B. *Shabbath* 10a

· VIII ·
ABOUT RIGHTEOUSNESS AND CHARITY

Imitatio Dei

Rabbi Ḥama, the son of Rabbi Ḥaninah, taught:

What is the meaning of "Follow none but the Lord your God, . . . and hold fast to Him" (Deuteronomy 13:5)? How can a human being follow and hold fast to a God of whom it is said that He is "a consuming fire" (Deuteronomy 4:24)?

"Following the Lord and holding fast to Him" can, therefore, only mean imitating His qualities.

He clothes the naked, as it is said in Genesis 3:21: "And the Lord God made for Adam and his wife garments of skin, and He clothed them." You, too, should clothe the naked!

The Holy One, praised be He, visited the sick, as it is said in Genesis 18:1: "The Lord appeared to him [Abraham] by the terebinths of Mamre, when he was sitting at the entrance of the tent as the day grew hot." (This happened while Abraham was recuperating from the effects of his circumcision. See Genesis 17:24.) You, too, should visit the sick!

The Holy One, praised be He, comforted the mourners, as it is said in Genesis 25:11: "After the death of Abraham, God blessed his son Isaac." You, too, should comfort the mourners!

The Holy One, praised be He, buried the dead, as it is said in

Deuteronomy 34:6: "He [the Lord] buried him [Moses] in the valley in the land of Moab." You, too, should bury the dead!

Rabbi Simlai explained:

The Torah begins with an act of kindness, and it concludes with an act of kindness. At the beginning it is written that God clothed Adam and Eve (Genesis 3:21). At the end it is written that He buried Moses (Deuteronomy 34:6).

B. *Sotah* 14a

"Charity Delivers from Death"

The Hebrew word *zedaqah,* which, in biblical Hebrew, has the sense of "righteousness" and, sometimes, "justification," acquired in rabbinic Hebrew the additional meaning of "charity." A Rabbi, reading a biblical text in which that word occurs, might be tempted to invest the biblical word with its rabbinic meaning—as was done with Proverbs 10:2 in the following passage.

Rabbi Judah used to say:

> *Ten hard things were created in the world.*
> *The rock is hard, but iron can split it.*
> *Iron is hard, but fire can soften it.*
> *Fire is hard, but water can extinguish it.*
> *Water is hard, but the clouds can bear it away.*
> *The clouds are hard, but the wind can scatter them.*
> *The wind is hard, but the human body can withstand it.*
> *The human body is hard, but fear can break it.*
> *Fear is hard, but wine can banish it.*
> *Wine is hard, but sleep can diminish its effect.*
> *Death is stronger than all,*
>   *but "Charity delivers from death."*

B. *Baba Bathra* 10a

The Times and Their Righteousness

Noah was a righteous man;
he was blameless in his age.
(Genesis 6:9)

Rabbi Yoḥanan said:
"In his age, Noah was a righteous man. But, if he had lived in a different, less wicked age, his righteousness would not have been so remarkable."
Resh Laqish said:
"If Noah managed to be righteous even in *his* age, how much more righteous would he have been had he lived in a different, less wicked age!"
Rabbi Ḥanina supplied an illustration in support of Rabbi Yoḥanan's view:
"This can be compared to a barrel of wine that is stored in a cellar together with vinegar. Compared to the vinegar, the wine has a good aroma. But if the wine were stored somewhere else, its aroma would not be considered nearly as good."
Rabbi Osha'ya supplied an illustration in support of the view of Resh Laqish:
"This can be compared to a vial of lavender oil that has been thrown upon the dunghill. If it smells good even there, how much better would it smell if it were lying among the spices!"

B. *Sanhedrin* 108a

Disappearance of Sins, Not of Sinners

In Rabbi Me-ir's neighborhood there lived some criminals, who annoyed him a great deal.

Rabbi Me-ir, therefore, prayed that they should die.

His wife, Beruriah, overheard this prayer, and she said to him: "How could you possibly think that such a prayer is even allowed? Is it because it says in Psalm 104:35, 'May sinners disappear from the earth, and the wicked be no more'? But the word that you take to mean 'sinners' (Hebrew: *ḥatta-im*) can also be read as 'sins' (Hebrew: *ḥata-im*). Just look at the second part of this verse, where it says, 'and the wicked be no more.' This means that, once there are no more sins, there will also be no more wicked people. You should rather be praying that those people repent; and then there will be no more wicked people around."

Rabbi Me-ir did so; and the criminals repented.

B. *Berakhoth* 10a

Why Rabbi Judah Suffered . . . , and Was Healed

A calf was once taken to be slaughtered. It escaped, hid its head under the cloak of Rabbi (Judah the Patriarch) and lowed in terror.

But Rabbi Judah pushed it away, saying: "Go! It was for this reason that you were created."

It was then said in heaven: "Since he has no pity, let Us bring sufferings upon him." . . .

(For thirteen years he suffered various diseases.)

One day, his maidservant was sweeping the house, and she chanced upon some young weasels lying there. She was about to sweep them out of the house, when Rabbi Judah stopped her, saying: "Let them be! It is written in Psalm 145:9: 'His mercy is upon all His works.' "

It was then said in heaven: "Since he is merciful, let Us be merciful to him."

(And that is why he was healed.)

B. *Baba Meẓi'a* 85a

Treasures in Heaven

Monobaz, King of Adiabene, together with his family, converted to Judaism in the first century C.E. Cf. Josephus, *Antiquities*, XX, ii, 1–4.)

Our Masters taught:

Once, in a time of famine, King Monobaz liberally dispersed among the poor his own wealth and the wealth accumulated by his ancestors.

His brothers and the family of his father banded together against him and berated him: "Your fathers have laid up treasures, and they have added to the treasures of their fathers. But you are squandering the accumulated wealth!"

Monobaz replied: "My fathers have laid up treasures here below, but I am laying them up above. . . . My fathers have laid up treasures in a place vulnerable to theft, but I have laid up treasures in a place not vulnerable to theft. . . . My fathers have laid up something that does not bear fruit, but I have laid up something that does bear fruit. . . . My fathers have laid up treasures of money, but I have laid up treasures of souls. . . . My fathers have laid up treasures for others, but I have laid up treasures for myself. . . . My fathers have laid up treasures for this world, but I have laid up treasures for the World-to-Come."

B. *Baba Bathra* 11a; cf. *Pesiqta Rabbathi*,
pisqa 25, ed. Friedmann, p. 126b;
Matthew 6:19–21; Luke 12:33–34; Mark 10:17–22

"Let Them All Enter Now!"

In a year of drought, Rabbi (Judah the Patriarch) once opened his storage chambers and proclaimed: "Whoever has studied Scripture and the various components of rabbinic law and lore may enter! But entrance is denied to the ignorant!"

Rabbi Jonathan ben Amram pushed his way in, and said: "Master, feed me!"

Rabbi Judah, who did not recognize him, asked him: "Have you studied the Scriptures?"

"No," answered Rabbi Jonathan.

"Have you studied rabbinic lore?"

"No."

"Then how can I give you food?"

"Feed me, then, like a dog, or as God feeds the ravens" (Psalm 147:9).

He gave him something to eat.

After Rabbi Jonathan had left, Rabbi Judah was bothered by his conscience: "Woe is me, for I have fed my bread to the ignorant!"

But his son, Rabbi Simeon, said to him: "Perhaps it was your disciple, Jonathan ben Amram. His whole life long he has refused to profit materially from the honor due the Torah."

Investigations were made, and it turned out that it had indeed been Rabbi Jonathan ben Amram.

Then Rabbi Judah said: "Let them all enter now!"

But Rabbi Judah had originally acted in accordance with his own stated principle. For Rabbi Judah had taught: "Misfortune comes into the world only because of the ignorant."

B. *Baba Bathra* 8a

Judge Not . . . !

Our Masters taught:

At one time, the Sages were in need of something that could only be arranged through the good offices of a certain noble Roman matron. That matron used to have liaisons with all the great ones of Rome.

The Sages asked: "Who of us is going to her?"

Rabbi Joshua volunteered.

Rabbi Joshua undertook the journey in the company of his disciples. When he came within four cubits of the matron's house, he removed his phylacteries. Then he entered the house and locked the door in the face of his disciples.

When he emerged again, he first went to a ritual bath, and only then did he study with his disciples.

He asked them: "What did you suspect me of, when I removed my phylacteries?"

They replied: "We thought that our Master was unwilling to take with him to a place of impurity the holy words contained in the phylacteries."

"And of what did you suspect me, when I locked the door in your faces?"

"We thought that, perhaps, our Master had to discuss some state secrets with the matron."

"And what did you suspect me of, when, later, I went to the ritual bath?"

"We thought that some of the matron's spittle had fallen on our Master's cloak, and that he had thus become ritually impure."

Then Rabbi Joshua cried out: "By the Temple cult! That is indeed how it was. And just as you have judged me favorably, so may the All-Present One judge you, too, favorably!"

B. *Shabbath* 127b

What He Usually Eats

A man once applied to Rabha for support.

Rabha asked him: "What do you usually eat?"

The man replied: "Fatted fowl and old wine."

Rabha asked: "Don't you give any thought to the burden that you impose upon the community?"

The man replied: "Do I eat of what belongs to the community? I eat of what belongs to the All-Merciful One! For it is said in Psalm 145:15: 'The eyes of all look to You, and You give them their food in due season.' (The Hebrew original permits the last three words to be understood as 'in his season.') Since it does not say here 'in *their* season,' but 'in *his* season,' it teaches us that the Holy One, praised be He, provides everyone with the kind of food that suits his own eating habits."

While that conversation was going on, Rabha's sister arrived. She had not seen her brother for thirteen years. As a gift she had brought him fatted fowl and old wine.

"Precisely what I have said!" the man exclaimed.

And Rabha said to him: "I ask for your forgiveness. Come and eat!"

B. *Kethubhoth* 67b

The Olive Leaf

*The dove came back to him toward evening,
and there in its bill was a
plucked-off olive leaf!*

(Genesis 8:11)

Whence did the dove bring that olive leaf?

Rabh Abba said: "From the young plants in the Land of Israel."

Rabbi Levi said: "From the Mount of Olives (in Jerusalem), for the Land of Israel was not inundated by the Flood."

Rabbi Berekhyah said: "The gates of Paradise were opened for the dove, and it brought the olive leaf from there."

But Rabbi Abbahu said: "If the dove really brought the olive leaf from Paradise, it could have brought something much better from there, like cinnamon or balsam. Yet it brought an olive leaf, in order to make Noah understand: 'Better something bitter from the hand of God than something sweet from your human hand!' "

Genesis Rabbah XXXIII, 6, ed. Theodor-Albeck,
p. 311; cf. *Leviticus Rabbah* XXXI, 10,
ed. Margulies, p. 732; b. *Sanhedrin* 108b

Dependent upon Your Hand Alone

Let us not be dependent,
O Lord our God,
upon the gifts of flesh and blood,
and not upon their loans;
but upon Your hand alone,
the full, open, overflowing and ample hand,
so that we may not be shamed nor confounded
forever and ever.

From the Jewish Grace after Meals

Those Who Love Him

They who suffer insult, but do not insult others,
who listen to reproach, but do not answer back,
who act out of love, and bear their pain in joy,
it is about them that Scripture says (Judges 5:31):

> *Those who love Him*
> *shall be like the sun*
> *as he rises in his might.*

B. *Shabbath* 88b; cf. b. *Gittin* 36b

Open the Gates!

When the Prophet Isaiah said (Isaiah 26:2): "Open the gates,"
he did *not* continue to say: "And let the priests, the Levites and the
Israelites enter." What he *did* say was: "And let a righteous *goy*
enter."

(The Hebrew word *goy* can mean "Gentile" as well as "nation.")

Siphra, Aḥaré Moth, 13:13, ed. Weiss, p. 86b

· IX ·
ABOUT HUSBAND
AND WIFE

Two Are Better Off Than One

Two are better off than one.
(Ecclesiastes 4:9)

This verse finds its explanation in Proverbs 18:22: "He who finds a wife finds a great good and obtains favor from the Lord."

But it is also said, in Ecclesiastes 7:26: "Now, I find woman more bitter than death."

What Scripture means to say, then, is this: If she is a good woman, there cannot be anything better; but if she is a bad woman, there cannot be anything worse.

This is the meaning of "He who finds a wife finds a great good."

You also find that, before woman was created, Scripture says: "It is not good for a man to be alone" (Genesis 2:18). But after she was created, it says: "And God saw all that He had made, and found it very good" (Genesis 1:31). Therefore: "He who finds a wife finds a great good."

Our Masters taught:
He who lives without a wife lives without blessing, without life, without joy, without help, without good and without peace.

"Without blessing," because it says in Genesis 11:28: "God

blessed them." "Them," the plural, shows that God bestowed His blessing only when there were two of them.

"Without life," because it says in Ecclesiastes 9:9: "Enjoy life with the woman you love."

"Without joy," because it says in Proverbs 5:18: "Rejoice in the wife of your youth."

"Without help," because it says in Genesis 2:18: "I will make a fitting helper for him."

"Without good," because it says in Proverbs 18:22: "He who finds a wife finds a great good."

"Without peace," because it says in Job 5:24: "You will know that there is peace in your tent," and the word *tent* means *wife,* as in Deuteronomy 5:27: "Return to your tents."

Some also say that a man who lives without a wife likewise lives without Torah. For it is said in Job 6:13: "If I have no help (i.e., wife) with me, then sound wisdom (i.e., Torah) is likewise driven from me."

This, then, is the meaning of: "He who finds a wife finds a great good." . . .

Indeed, so important is matrimony that the Holy One, praised be He, links His name to marriage in all three parts of Scripture— in the Pentateuch, in the Prophets and in the Hagiographa.

In the Pentateuch, for it is written in Genesis 24:50, when Eliezer brought Rebecca to be Isaac's wife: "Then Laban and Bethuel answered, 'The matter stems from the Lord.' "

In the Prophets, for it is written in Judges 14:4 (a book that, in the Hebrew Scriptures, belongs to the prophetic canon) about Samson's choice of a wife: "His father and his mother did not realize that this was the Lord's doing."

And in the Hagiographa, for it is written in Proverbs 19:14: "A prudent wife is from the Lord."

You learn from this that the Holy One, praised be He, links His name to marriage.

Midrash Tehillim LIX, 2, ed. S. Buber, pp. 151a,b

Rabbi Ele'azar said: "Any man who does not have a wife is not a complete human being; for it is said in Genesis 5:2: 'Male and female He created them. And when they were created, He blessed them and called them Man.' "

B. *Yebhamoth* 63a

Difficult as
the Splitting of the Sea

A Roman matron asked Rabbi Yossé ben Ḥalaphta: "In how many days did God create the world?"

He answered: "In six days; for thus it is written in Exodus 31:17: 'In six days the Lord made heaven and earth.' "

"And what has He done since?"

"He unites the couples and arranges the marriages. He decides whose daughter is to marry whom."

"But that," remarked the matron, "is something that even I can do! I own many manservants and many maidservants, and I can couple them quite easily."

To which Rabbi Yossé replied: "You might consider this to be an easy thing. Yet for God this task is as difficult as the splitting of the Sea of Reeds."

Rabbi Yossé went on his way. The Roman matron, for her part, had a row of one thousand manservants confront a row of one thousand maidservants. Then she commanded: "So-and-so is going to marry so-and-so; and so-and-so is going to marry so-and-so!" This was to happen that very night.

The next morning, the couples thus paired appeared before the matron—one with a smashed skull, another with a missing eye, a third with a broken leg. This one said: "I do not like that woman!" That one said: "I cannot stand this man!"

The Roman matron sent for Rabbi Yossé ben Ḥalaphta and said to him: "Your Torah is absolutely right; and what you have told me is really true!"

But Rabbi Yossé merely replied: "That is what I have been telling you. You might consider the arranging of marriages to be an easy task. But for God it is as difficult as the splitting of the Sea of Reeds."

> *Pesiqta deRabh Kahana, pisqa* 2, ed. S. Buber,
> pp. 11b–12a; cf. *Genesis Rabbah* LXVIII, 4,
> ed. Theodor-Albeck, pp. 771–73; *Leviticus
> Rabbah* VIII, 1, ed. Margulies, pp. 164–66

Chercher la Femme

His disciples asked Rabbi Dosethai, the son of Rabbi Yannai: "Why is it the man who goes in search of the woman, and not the woman who goes in search of the man?"

He answered with a parable:

"A man loses something. Who is looking for what? Obviously, he who has lost something is looking for that which he has lost! (And Eve was made out of Adam's 'lost' rib.)"

> B. *Niddah* 31b

The Rib

Rabbi Joshua of Sikhnin taught in the name of Rabbi Levi:

Before God created Eve, He first sought to determine from what part of Adam's anatomy He should create her.

He said: "I shall not create her from his head, so that she will not become light-headed. I shall not create her from his eye, so that she will not become a flirt; nor from his ear, so that she will not become an eavesdropper; and not from his mouth, so that she will not become a gossip. I shall not create her from his heart, so that she will not become jealous; not from his hand, so that she will not be thievish; and not from his foot, so that she will not become a gadabout. But I shall create her from a modest part of Adam's body, from a part that will always remain covered—even when he stands naked."

He therefore created her from Adam's rib. And over every limb that He created, He repeated the words: "Be a chaste woman! Be a chaste woman!"

Nevertheless, as it is written: "But you have ignored My counsel and would have none of My reproof" (Proverbs 1:25). . . . All the qualities that God had sought to withhold from the woman are fully exemplified by her.

Genesis Rabbah XVIII, 2, ed. Theodor-Albeck,
pp. 162–63; cf. *Midrash Tanḥuma, Wayyeshebh,* 6

The Choice

Our Masters taught:
If one has the choice between studying the Torah and marrying, one should first study and then marry.

But if someone finds it impossible to live without a wife, let him first marry and then study.

Rabh Judah said in the name of Samuel: "The decision is that a man should first marry and then study."

Rabbi Yoḥanan objected: "With a millstone around one's neck, how could one possibly devote oneself to the study of the Torah?"

But there really is no difference of opinion. What Rabh Judah taught in the name of Samuel refers to us Babylonians. What Rabbi Yoḥanan said refers to the Palestinian students.

B. *Qiddushin* 29b

Lentils and Peas

Rabh was constantly vexed by his wife. When he asked her for lentils, she cooked peas for him; and when he asked for peas, she cooked lentils for him.

When his son, Ḥiyya, grew up, he would change his father's instructions into their opposite before transmitting them to his mother.

Rabh now received what he asked for; and he once said to his son: "Your mother has improved."

But his son informed him that it was he who had been changing the instructions.

Rabh said to him: "This is what people mean when they say: 'Your own children teach you reason.' " But he also admonished him: "You must no longer do so, lest you be subject to the Prophet's accusation: 'They have trained their tongues to speak falsely; they wear themselves out working iniquity' " (Jeremiah 9:4).

B. *Yebhamoth* 63a

The Foiled Divorce

It once happened that a certain woman in Sidon lived with her husband for ten years without giving birth to a child. Following the law that, in those days, governed such matters, they went to Rabbi Simeon ben Yoḥai to arrange for a divorce.

The Rabbi said to them: "By your life! Just as you had a festive banquet when you got married, so you should not separate now without first having a festive banquet."

They followed the Rabbi's advice and prepared a great banquet.

During that banquet, the woman gave her husband more to drink than usual. When he was in high spirits, he said to his wife:

"Little daughter, you may take with you out of my house whatever you like best; and then return to the house of your father."

What did she do?

After he had fallen sound asleep, she ordered her manservants and her maidservants to take him and the bed upon which he was sleeping to her father's house.

About midnight the man awoke. When his intoxication had worn off, he looked around in astonishment. "Little daughter," he said, "where am I?"

"You are," she replied, "in my father's house."

"But what business do I have in your father's house?"

She replied: "Don't you remember your telling me last night that I may take with me whatever I like best when I return to my father's house? Nothing in the whole world do I like better than you!"

They then went again to Rabbi Simeon bar Yoḥai. The Rabbi prayed for her, and the woman became pregnant.

Canticles Rabbah I, 4, ii

Peace between Husband and Wife

Rabbi Me-ir was in the habit of delivering discourses on Sabbath evenings. Among his listeners there was a certain woman.

Once the discourse took a very long time, and the woman stayed until the end. When she returned home, she found that the light had already gone out. Angrily her husband wanted to know: "Where have you been?"

She replied: "I sat listening to a preacher."

Her husband now adjured her, saying: "You are forbidden to enter this house until you have spat in the preacher's face!"

She stayed away from home one week, two weeks, three weeks. Finally her neighbors said to her: "Are you still quarreling? Come, let us go with you to the preacher."

When Rabbi Me-ir saw her coming, he was able, through the

gift of the Holy Spirit, to understand the whole sequence of events.

He said: "My eye hurts. Is there, perhaps, among you an understanding woman, capable of whispering a charm over my eye?"

Now the woman's neighbors said to her: "If you were to go and spit into his eye, you would be able to annul your husband's adjuration."

The woman went, and sat down in front of Rabbi Me-ir. But she was afraid of him, and she said. "Rabbi, I really have no experience in whispering charms over eyes."

But the Rabbi said: "Nevertheless, do spit in my face seven times! Then I shall be healed."

She did so.

After that, Rabbi Me-ir said to the woman: "Go home now, and tell your husband: 'You demanded of me to spit in the preacher's face once; I have done it seven times!' "

After the woman had left, his disciples said to Rabbi Me-ir: "Is it proper to let the Torah be brought into such contempt? Could you not simply have asked one of us to whisper a charm over your eye?"

But Rabbi Me-ir replied: "Is it not fitting for Me-ir to attempt to imitate his Creator? For Rabbi Ishmael had taught: Great is peace, because the Name of God, though written down in holiness, was, according to the divine commandment (Numbers 5:11–31), to be blotted out in water, if only peace could thereby be restored between husband and wife!"

Leviticus Rabbah IX, 9, ed. Margulies,
pp. 191–93; cf. p. *Sotah* I, 4,
ed. Krotoshin, p. 16d; *Numbers Rabbah* IX, 20

The Bald Head

Rabh Ammi and Rabh Assi were once sitting before Rabbi Isaac the Blacksmith. One said to him: "May the Master teach us legal traditions!" And the other said to him: "May the Master teach us narrative traditions!"

When Rabbi Isaac began to teach narrative traditions, he was interrupted by the one. But when he began to teach legal traditions, he was interrupted by the other.

Finally, Rabbi Isaac said to them: "I will tell you a parable. To what may our situation be compared? To a man who had two wives, a young one and an old one. The young wife pulled out his white hair, and the old one pulled out his black hair. In the end, the poor man was left with no hair at all, having been made bald on both sides."

B. *Baba Qamma* 60b

"You Preach Well!"

It was taught:

Rabbi Eli'ezer said: He who does not fulfill the commandment of procreation is as though he had shed blood. For it is said in Genesis 9:6: "Whoever sheds the blood of man, by man shall his blood be shed." And in the very next verse (Genesis 9:7) it says: "Be fertile, then, and increase!"

Rabbi Jacob said: He is as though he had diminished the Divine Image, for Genesis 9:6 continues by saying: "In the image of God was man created." And the very next verse (Genesis 9:7) says: "Be fertile, then, and increase!"

Ben 'Azzai, who himself was a bachelor, noting that "Be fertile, then, and increase!" follows upon *both* "Whoever sheds the blood of man" *and* "In the image of God was man created," argued that he who does not fulfill the commandment of procreation is as though he had shed blood *and* diminished the Divine Image.

His colleagues said to him: "Some people preach well and do well what they preach. Some do well, but are unable to preach well. You, however, preach well, but are unable to do what you preach!"

Ben 'Azzai replied: "What can I do? My soul is in love with the Torah. Perhaps the survival of the world can be entrusted to others."

B. *Yebhamoth* 63b

Epithalamion

Our Masters taught:

What does one sing when one is dancing before the bride?

The School of Shammai said: "One describes the bride as she really looks."

The School of Hillel said: "One sings: 'Beautiful and graceful bride!' "

The Shammaites said to the Hillelites: "Is one really to sing of her 'Beautiful and graceful bride!' even if she is lame or blind? After all, the Torah says: 'Keep far from a false matter!' " (Exodus 23:7).

The Hillelites answered: "If someone has made a bad deal at the marketplace, should one, according to your opinion, praise or deprecate in his presence the purchase he has made? Surely, even you would admit that, in order to spare his feelings, one should praise it in his presence!"

On the basis of this principle, the Sages had also said: "A man should always try to be pleasant in his dealings with others."

When Rabh Dimi came from Palestine to Babylonia, he related that, in Palestine, they sing, when dancing before the bride:

> *She uses no powder, and she uses no paint.*
> *She does not get her hair dyed.*
> *Yet she looks like a graceful gazelle!*

B. *Kethubhoth* 16b, 17a

• X •
ABOUT MIRACLES
AND MERITS

Why Moses Stammered

After the boy Moses had been brought into Pharaoh's palace (Exodus 2:10), Pharaoh's daughter would hug and kiss him. She loved him as though he were her own son, and she would not let him leave the royal palace. Because he was so handsome, everybody wanted to see him; and whoever saw him could not tear himself away from him again.

Pharaoh himself used to embrace him and kiss him. On such occasions, Moses would take the crown off Pharaoh's head and place it upon his own head. In a certain sense, he was, after all, destined to do so, once he was grown up. . . .

But the magicians of Egypt sat there and did not like what they saw. They said to Pharaoh: "We are afraid of him who is taking the crown off your head and placing it upon his own head. He could well be the one of whom we prophesied that he will tear the kingdom away from you."

Some of the magicians now counseled Pharaoh to have Moses slain. Others preferred to have him burnt.

Jethro, too, was among the counselors, and he said: "This boy has no sense. Simply put him to the test! Place in front of him a golden vessel and a burning coal. If he reaches for the gold, then he has sense, and you should have him slain. But if he reaches for the burning coal, he obviously has no sense, and then he does not deserve capital punishment."

The advice was accepted. They placed the golden vessel and the burning coal in front of Moses. He was just about to reach for the golden vessel, when the angel Gabriel appeared and pushed Moses' hand away from the gold. Moses grasped the burning coal, instead, and put it into his mouth. He burnt his tongue, and thus he became, as Scripture says (Exodus 4:10), "slow of speech and slow of tongue."

Exodus Rabbah I, 26

Fated

King Solomon had a very beautiful daughter, like whom there was no other in the whole Land of Israel.

Solomon observed the constellations in order to discover who would be fated to become his daughter's husband. He saw that it would be a very poor man, whose poverty was unmatched by anyone else's in all of Israel.

What did King Solomon do?

He had a high tower built in the midst of the sea in such a way that the sea surrounded the tower on all sides. Then he took his daughter and locked her up in this high tower. He detailed seventy of the Elders of Israel to be her attendants, and he supplied the tower with ample provisions. The tower had no entrance, and nobody could enter it. Then Solomon said: "Now I will see 'the work of God and His deed' " (Psalms 64:10).

After a while it happened that the poor man, who was fated to become the husband of Solomon's daughter, was traveling at night. He had no clothes, and he was barefoot, hungry and thirsty. He also had no place where he could spend the night. Then he saw the carcass of an ox, which had been thrown away onto a field. He climbed inside it, to protect himself from the cold, and he fell asleep.

Now a giant bird swooped down upon the carcass, carried it off, and deposited it upon the roof of the tower in which King Solomon's daughter lived. There, the bird consumed the flesh still attached to the carcass. But, when the morning dawned, the young man found himself on the roof.

It was the habit of Solomon's daughter to climb up to the roof every day. When she did it now, she saw the young man. She asked him: "Who are you? And who brought you here?"

He replied: "I am a Jew from Acco. A bird has brought me here."

What did she do?

She took him, brought him into her chamber, washed him, rubbed him with oil and dressed him. She discovered that he was a very handsome man, the like of whom was not to be found in the whole territory of Israel. The young man was also very learned, and he had a keen mind. He was a scholar. The young lady fell in love with him, and her soul was cleaving to his.

One day she asked him: "Would you like to marry me?"

And he replied: "Oh, if only I could!"

What did he do?

He opened one of his veins, and with his own blood he wrote the document of marriage demanded by law. Then he recited the wedding formula, and he called out: "God and the angels Michael and Gabriel are my witnesses today!" After that, he conducted himself with her as is customary among people under those circumstances.

She became pregnant.

When the Elders saw her in that condition, they said to her: "It would appear to us that you are pregnant."

She admitted it.

Then the Elders asked: "And from whom are you pregnant?"

She replied: "What business is that of yours?"

The Elders now made long faces, for they were afraid that King Solomon might suspect one of them in this matter. They, therefore, invited the King to come and talk with them. The King went aboard a ship, and he came to the Elders.

The Elders said to him: "Your Majesty, such-and-such is the situation. But let Your Majesty not accuse his servants!"

Solomon now had his daughter brought to him, and he asked her what had happened. The daughter replied: "The Holy One, praised be He, has sent me this young man. He is handsome and good, and he is a great scholar. He married me according to the provisions of our religious law." Then she called for the young man.

He came before the King and showed him the document of marriage that he had written for the King's daughter. The King now questioned him about his father, about his mother, about his family and about his native city. From the young man's answers the King could see that this was indeed the young man who had been indicated to him by the stars.

The King was very happy, and he said: "Praised be the All-Present One, who gives us what is meant for us, and of whom it is said (in Psalm 68:7): 'He restores the lonely to their homes and sets free the imprisoned, safe and sound'!"

From a *Tanḥuma* manuscript, published by S. Buber in the Introduction to his edition of *Midrash Tanḥuma,* p. 68b

Healing

Rabbi Alexandri taught in the name of Rabbi Ḥiyya bar Abba:

Greater is the miracle that happens when the sick are healed than the miracle that happened to Hananiah, Mishael and Azariah (cf. Daniel, chapters 1–3).

The fire, from which Hananiah, Mishael and Azariah were saved, was a fire kindled by human beings. Human beings kindle it, and human beings can extinguish it again.

But sickness is a fire kindled by God. Who, then, could presume to be able to extinguish it?

B. *Nedarim* 41a

The Greeting from
the Heavenly Academy

According to a rabbinic notion, the scholars who die are merely transferred from the earthly to the Heavenly Academy, at which latter they continue to study the Torah, their instructor being God Himself.

Abba the Bloodletter used to receive a daily greeting from the Heavenly Academy.

But the learned Abbaye received such a greeting only every Friday.

And the learned Rabha received it only once a year, on the eve of the Day of Atonement.

Abbaye felt slighted because Abba the Bloodletter received the higher distinction. But Abbaye was informed: "You cannot perform the kind of deeds performed by Abba!"

What were the deeds of Abba the Bloodletter?

When he performed the operation of bloodletting, he had two separate consulting rooms, one for men and one for women. He also used a garment with many openings, which he asked his women patients to put on, so that he was not compelled to look upon their naked bodies. Outside his consulting room he had placed a box into which his patients deposited the fees. Those who had money paid there. Those who did not have money could leave the house without being embarrassed. And when Abba dealt with someone who could not pay at all, he would actually give him money and say: "Go, strengthen yourself!"

One day, Abbaye sent a pair of scholars to Abba the Bloodletter in order to discover the truth about him. When they had come to his house, he gave them food and beverage, and he placed in front of them pillows on which they could sleep.

The next morning, the scholars took the pillows with them and brought them to the marketplace. Abbaye then sent for Abba, and the scholars asked him to estimate the price of the pillows. Abba mentioned a certain sum, but the scholars wondered: "Perhaps they are worth more than this?"

"No," said Abba. "This is what I have paid for them myself."

Then the scholars asked him: "Of what did you suspect us?"

Abba answered: "I thought that the scholars were in need of the money for some charitable purpose, but were ashamed to tell me so."

The scholars now said to Abba: "Take the pillows back!"

But he replied: "No. This I cannot do. For, from the moment when I no longer paid any attention to them, I regarded them as devoted to charity."

B. *Ta'anith* 21b, 22a

The Table Leg That Was Taken Back

Rabbi Ḥanina ben Dossa was very poor.

One day, Rabbi Ḥanina's wife said to him: "Why don't you pray that some of the good, which is stored for the righteous in the World-to-Come, be given to us already here?"

He prayed.

Then the leg of a golden table was hurled into their house.

But he saw in a dream that, in the World-to-Come, all would eat at tables with three legs. His table, however, only had two legs.

He told the dream to his wife, and she begged him: "Please pray that the golden table leg be taken back!"

He prayed; and the golden table leg was taken back.

It was taught:

The second miracle was even greater than the first. According to a tradition, it is indeed possible that one be granted that for which one has prayed. But that which has been given is never taken back.

B. *Ta'anith* 25a

His Merits Are Very Great

In Neharde'a there stood a ruined wall that Rabh and Samuel would never pass, even though the wall had already stood in its ruined state for thirteen years.

One day Rabh Adda bar Ahabhah came to that place. When they reached the vicinity of the wall, Samuel suggested to Rabh that they make their customary detour. But Rabh replied: "That is unnecessary now. Rabh Adda bar Ahabhah is with us. His merits are very great, and they will protect us. Therefore I am not afraid."

Rabh Huna had stored wine in a ruined house, and he now wanted to remove it from there. He, therefore, involved Rabh Adda bar Ahabhah in a discussion about matters of religious law until all the wine had been removed. As soon as they had left the house, the house fell in.

When Rabh Adda bar Ahabhah became aware of the purpose for which he had been used, he grew angry. He said: "Is not this a case like the one about which Rabbi Yannai had said that one must never stay in a place of danger, believing that one would be saved by a miracle? Perhaps no miracle will happen. And even if a miracle does happen, it will be deducted from one's merits."

B. *Ta'anith* 20b

The Miracle Was Too Small

A pestilence once broke out in Sura, but the neighborhood of Rabh was spared. People thought that this was due to Rabh's merit. But they were informed in a dream that the miracle was too small to be attributed to Rabh's great merit.

The miracle was to be attributed to the merits of a man who lent his hoe and his shovel to a cemetery, so that graves could be dug.

* * *

A conflagration once broke out in Doqereth, but the neighborhood of Rabh Huna was spared. People thought that this was due to Rabh Huna's merit. But they were informed in a dream that the miracle was too small to be attributed to Rabh Huna's great merit.

The miracle was to be attributed to the merit of a certain woman who used to heat her own oven and place it at the disposal of her neighbors.

B. *Ta'anith* 21b

Grace

I will be gracious to whom I will be gracious,
and show compassion to whom I will show compassion.
(Exodus 33:19)

At that time, the Holy One, praised be He, showed Moses all the treasure chambers of heaven, in which the reward of the righteous is stored.

Moses asked Him: "Sovereign of the Universe, for whom is this treasure chamber intended?"

God replied: "For those who lead a righteous life."

"And that treasure chamber?"

"For people who support orphans."

The conversation continued for a while, as Moses was shown a number of other treasure chambers and informed about the prospective recipients.

Then they came to an enormous treasure chamber.

Moses asked: "And for whom is this treasure chamber intended?"

God replied: "If someone has his own merits, I give to him from the particular treasure chamber intended for him. But if someone has no merit of his own, then I give him freely (i.e., graciously) from this treasure chamber."

* * *

That is why it is written: "I will be gracious to whom I will be gracious."

Midrash Tanḥuma, Ki Thissa, 16,
ed. S. Buber, p. 58b; cf. *Exodus Rabbah* 45:6

For the Sake of the Small Cattle

When Alexander the Great came to North Africa, the local inhabitants brought to him golden apples, golden pomegranates and golden loaves of bread. But he said to them: "I did not come to you in order to take a look at your wealth, but in order to familiarize myself with your laws."

Just then two men came before the African king, and they demanded his verdict.

One man said: "Your Majesty! I have bought a carob tree from this man here. When I scraped it, I found a treasure in it. I, therefore, asked the man to take back the treasure, because I have bought the carob tree only, not the treasure that is hidden in it. But the man refuses to take it back."

The other man now said: "Just as you are afraid of punishment, so am I afraid of punishment. When I sold you the carob tree, I sold it to you together with everything that is on it and in it."

The African king then asked the one man: "Do you have a son?"

He replied: "Yes."

Then he asked the other man: "Do you have a daughter?"

He replied: "Yes."

"In that case," said the king, "your children ought to marry each other and enjoy the treasure together!"

Alexander the Great was amazed.

"Why are you amazed?" asked the African king. "Did I not render a just verdict?"

"Of course, you did," answered Alexander.

The African king continued: "If this case had occurred in your own country, how would you have decided it?"

Alexander replied: "Both men would have lost their heads, and the treasure would have found its way into the royal treasury."

"Tell me," the African king said, "does the sun shine in your country?"

"Yes," replied Alexander.

"Does the rain fall in your country?"

"Yes."

"Do you, perhaps, have small cattle in your country?"

"Of course."

"Now I can understand why the sun shines and the rain falls in your country. It is not on account of your righteousness that you are saved, but for the sake of the small cattle!"

That is why it is said in Psalm 36:7: "Man and beast You save, O Lord." This means: You, O Lord, are saving man because of the merits of the beasts.

> *Leviticus Rabbah* XXVII, 1, ed. Margulies,
> pp. 618–23; cf. *Midrash Tanḥuma,*
> *Emor,* 9, ed. S. Buber, pp. 44b–45a

· XI ·
ABOUT REDEMPTION AND THE WORLD-TO-COME

When Will the Son of David Come?

Rabbi Yoḥanan said:

If you see a generation increasingly dwindling away, hope for the Messiah. For thus it is written in 2 Samuel 22:28: "The afflicted people You will save."

Rabbi Yoḥanan also said:

If you see a generation overflooded by many troubles as a stream, hope for the Messiah. For thus it is written in Isaiah 59:19: "When the enemy will come like a rushing stream that the wind of the Lord drives on. . . ." And immediately afterward (Isaiah 59:20) it says: "And a Redeemer shall come unto Zion."

Rabbi Yoḥanan said furthermore:

The son of David will come only in a generation that is wholly righteous, or in a generation that is wholly wicked. . . .

Rabbi Alexandri pointed out a contradiction in Isaiah 60:22. There, speaking about the messianic redemption, Scripture says: "I the Lord will speed it in its time."

Now, if it is to be "in its time," what is the meaning of "I the Lord will speed it"? But if the Lord "will speed it," what is the meaning of "in its time"?

But Rabbi Alexandri also showed that this was not really a true contradiction. He explained: If Israel is worthy, then "I the Lord will speed it." But if Israel is not worthy, then redemption will come only "in its (predetermined) time."

B. *Sanhedrin* 98a

"Today"

One day, Rabbi Joshua ben Levi asked the Prophet Elijah: "When will the Messiah come?"

Elijah answered: "Go to him and ask him himself!"

Rabbi Joshua wanted to know: "But where is he?"

Elijah replied: "At the gates of Rome."

"And how shall I recognize him?"

"He is sitting among the poor lepers. But, while all the others take off all their bandages at once and put them on again all together, the Messiah takes off his bandages one after the other and puts them on again one after the other. For he thinks that God might call him at any minute to bring redemption, and he, therefore, holds himself in a state of constant preparedness."

Rabbi Joshua went to him, and greeted him: "Peace be upon you, my Master and Teacher!"

And the Messiah replied: "Peace be upon you, son of Levi!"

"When will the Master come?"

"Today!" . . .

Later, Rabbi Joshua complained to the Prophet Elijah: "The Messiah has lied to me. He said that he was coming today; but he did not come."

Elijah answered: "You did not understand him correctly. He was quoting Psalm 95:7 to you: 'Today, if you will but hearken to His voice!' "

B. *Sanhedrin* 98a

The Light

Rabbi Yoḥanan preached on Psalm 36:10.

With You is the fountain of life;
by Your light do we see light.

It once happened that a man lit a lantern and walked on his way. But the light went out. He rekindled the lantern; but it again went out. This happened again and again. Whenever he rekindled the lantern, the light went out again.

Finally the man said to himself: "How long am I going to tire myself out with this lantern? I shall wait until the sun is shining, and then I shall walk in the light of the sun."

So, too, did things go with the Israelites. They were enslaved in Egypt. Then Moses arose and liberated them. But Babylon enslaved them again. Then Daniel, Hananiah, Mishael and Azariah arose and liberated them. But they were again enslaved in Elam, Media and Persia. Then Mordecai and Esther arose and liberated them. After that, they were enslaved by Hellas; but the Maccabees redeemed them. And now they are enslaved by wicked Rome.

Today the Israelites are saying: "Now we are tired of being slaves and being redeemed, of being slaves and being redeemed. Let us no longer pray for redemption by mere flesh and blood, but only for the redemption by our Redeemer, the Lord of hosts, who is called the Holy One of Israel. Now let us no longer pray that mere flesh and blood give us light, but only that the Holy One, praised be He, give us light."

That is why it is said: "With You is the fountain of life; by Your light do we see light." And it is said: "The Lord is God; He has given us light" (Psalm 118:27).

Midrash Tehillim 36:6, ed. S. Buber, p. 125b

Who Will Enter
the Kingdom of Heaven?

Rabbi Baruqa of Ḥuza often went to the marketplace at Lapet.

One day, the Prophet Elijah appeared to him there; and Rabbi Baruqa asked him: "Is there anyone among all these people who will have a share in the World-to-Come?"

Elijah answered: "There is none."

. . .

Later, two men came to the marketplace; and Elijah said to Rabbi Baruqa: "Those two will have a share in the World-to-Come!"

Rabbi Baruqa asked the newcomers: "What is your occupation?"

They replied: "We are clowns. When we see someone who is sad, we cheer him up. When we see two people quarreling, we try to make peace between them."

B. *Ta'anith* 22a

Dying and Destined to Live Again

Rabbi Ele'azar Haqappar used to say:

Those who are born are destined to die.
Those who are dead are destined to live again.
Those who will live again are destined to be judged—
to know, to make known and to be made aware
that He is God, He is the Maker, He is the Creator,
He is the Discerner, He is the Judge, the Witness and the Claimant.
He, praised be He, will ultimately give the verdict.
With Him there is no iniquity,

no forgetfulness,
no respect of persons,
and no taking of bribes.

Know, therefore, that all is according to the reckoning.
Let not your evil inclination mislead you into thinking
that the grave will be a place of refuge for you.
For without your will you were created,
without your will you were born,
without your will you live,
without your will you die,
and without your will you are destined
to give an account and a reckoning
before the Supreme King of Kings,
The Holy One, praised be He.

Mishnah Abhoth 4:22

This World and the Next

Rabbi Jacob used to say:
This world is like an entrance hall of the World-to-Come. Prepare yourself in the entrance hall, so that you may be allowed to enter the banquet hall.

He also used to say:
Better is one hour of repentance and good deeds in this world than the whole of the life in the World-to-Come. But better is one hour of equanimity in the World-to-Come than the whole of life in this world.

Mishnah Abhoth 4:16–17

No Rest

Rabh Ḥiyya bar Ashi said in the name of Rabh:
The scholars have no rest—either in this world or in the next.
For thus it is said in Psalm 84:8: "They go from strength to
strength, appearing before God in Zion."

B. *Berakhoth* 64a

Not Like This World

This was a favorite saying of Rabh's:

> *Not like this world is the World-to-Come.*
> *In the World-to-Come*
> *there is no eating or drinking,*
> *no procreation, no business and no envy,*
> *no hatred, and no competition.*
>> *But the righteous are sitting*
>> *with crowns on their heads,*
>> *delighting in the radiance of the Divine Presence*

B. *Berakhoth* 17a; cf. Mark 12:25; Matthew 22:30; also
Matthew 19:28

No Eye Has Seen It

Rabbi Ḥiyya bar Abba said in the name of Rabbi Yoḥanan:
All the prophecies of the Prophets concerning the future refer
exclusively to the (thisworldly) Days of the Messiah. But with
regard to the World-to-Come, Isaiah 64:3 applies: "No eye has
seen it, O God, but You, who act for those who trust in You."

B. *Berakhoth* 34b; cf. b. *Sanhedrin* 99a

SCRIPTURE VERSES QUOTED OR REFERRED TO

(a) Hebrew Bible

115

(b) New Testament